david olshine

STUDIES ON THE GO

JAMES
1-2 PETER
1-3 JOHN

ZONDERVAN®

youth
specialties

ZONDERVAN

James, 1-2 Peter, and 1-3 John
Copyright © 2014 by David B. Olshine

YS Youth Specialties is a trademark of Real Resources Incorporated and is registered with the United States Patent and Trademark Office.

This title is also available as a Zondervan ebook.
Visit www.zondervan.com/ebooks.

Requests for information should be addressed to:

Zondervan, 3900 *Sparks Dr. SE, Grand Rapids, Michigan 49546*

Library of Congress Cataloging-in-Publication Data

Olshine, David, 1954–
    James, 1-2 Peter, and 1-3 John / David Olshine.
      pages cm. – (Studies on the go)
    ISBN 978-0-310-51677-4 (softcover)
    1. Bible. James – Study and teaching. 2. Bible. Peter – Study and teaching. 3. Bible. Epistles of John – Study and teaching. 4. Christian education of children. I. Title.
BS2785.55.O47 2014
227'.90071–dc23
                                                  2014024081

Cover design: Toolbox Studios
Interior design: SharpSeven Design/David Conn

Printed in the United States of America

HB 02.26.2018

DEDICATION

To my mom, who encouraged me in middle school that I was made to be a communicator.

To June and Chick: You have modeled love, perseverance, and determination.

To the great folks who make up Columbia International University: Staff, faculty, and students.

A special shout out goes to the Youth Ministry, Family, and Culture (YMFC) team at CIU: Sam Rubinson, Karen Grant, Megan Bentley, and our dean, John Harvey.

To all the past, present, and future YMFC students: "Live the dream."

To Sandhills Community, one of the most grace-filled churches I have been able to do ministry with: I am honored to serve on the teaching team.

To my buddy Larry Wagner: Words cannot express the admiration, love, and respect I have for you. You are resilient. And you do it all so humbly, trusting God for his will.

To my wife and soul mate Rhonda Lee Olshine: After three decades of marriage, it just keeps getting better and better.

To my children, Rachel and Andrew: I cannot imagine life without you. You are the apple of my eye.

CONTENTS

Part 3: The Letters of First, Second, and Third John

HOW TO USE STUDIES ON THE GO

Maybe you've tried to lead a study and ended up not knowing what to say or where to take the lesson. These studies have all of the best ingredients for helping students and adults connect with God and each other as they encounter Scripture. The studies work best in a small group or intimate format, but can also be utilized in Bible studies, Sunday school, youth group—even road trips and retreats.

Before each of the three sections you'll find some Handy Tips and Insights: These introductory sections help the leader or facilitator know some of the historical background and purpose of each letter.

Each session is then broken up into the following subsections:

- Leader's Insight: An overview of each session to help the leader or facilitator understand the background and focus of the text.

- Share (Warm-Up Questions): All groups need a common ground before they break ground into the Bible. The questions are usually light and user friendly. The goal here is to help your group relax so they can engage with God's Word.

- Observe (Observation Questions): These help the novice or veteran focus on what the passage says. The goal is to *bring to the surface what the students are noticing about the passage. The intent is to observe.*

- Think (Interpretation Questions): These help your group consider what the author meant when he wrote the letters. The goal is to discover what the writer was saying to his audience, then and now.

- Apply (Application Questions): These focus on helping the group connect God's truth to their own lives.

- Do: An activity option that helps students apply God's truth. The goal here is *action*—putting head knowledge into real-life application.

- Quiet Time Reflections: One reproducible handout page for each session providing exercises to help students personally reflect on the passages on a daily basis.

My hope is that these studies create an environment where students and adults experience community and are valued and respected. The leader's job is to facilitate a safe place where people can be known and be authentic.

The worst kind of small group occurs when the leader does all the talking and the students sit and stare with a glazed look on their faces. The best small groups are fluid yet organized, with a free-flowing exchange of conversation. This type of group encourages each person to share his or her thoughts and ideas.

May God bless you as you engage students in the process of applying God's truth to their hearts and minds.

And thanks for picking up this book.

—*David Olshine*

Part 1

The Book of James

HANDY INSIGHTS AND TIPS ON THE BOOK OF JAMES

WHO? James is the author of this book (James 1:1), and we need to ask, "Who is James?" There are five men named James in the New Testament. Most scholars believe the writer of this book was the half-brother of Jesus. He was a biological son of Joseph and Mary. We read in John 7:5 that when James was growing up, he didn't believe Jesus was the Messiah. After his resurrection, Jesus appeared to more than 500 people, and one of the first was James (1 Corinthians 15:7). This life-changing event ignited James' personal journey with Jesus. He begins his letter as, "James, a servant of God and of the Lord Jesus Christ." (1:1) James doesn't refer to himself as Jesus' half-brother; rather he says he's a servant of the *Lord Jesus Christ*. Jesus is now in charge of James' life, which results in this letter explaining what it means to follow Christ.

WHERE? James was a Jewish follower of Jesus, and he addresses his book to the "twelve tribes scattered among the nations" (verse 1), a reference to Jewish believers in Jesus persecuted for their faith. These believers were displaced, battled discouragement, and needed words of hope and faith.

WHEN? Many scholars believe the book of James was written between A.D. 45-49 and prior to the Jerusalem council meeting, which took place in A.D. 50. Some believe James was written about A.D. 45, which would make it the *oldest book* in the New Testament.

WHAT? The Book of James is declaring that we don't get to heaven by good works, but by God's grace. We don't do good deeds to become more Christ-like; we do good deeds because we *are* Christ-like.

Reading the Bible should not be passive but active, and that's why James challenges his readers to care for widows, guard our words, and pray for the sick. Faith in Christ is always dynamic and proactive. True faith produces good works. That is the message of James.

A simple outline to teach students the flow of James:

- James 1—Trials and Temptation
- James 2—Faith and Works
- James 3—Taming the Tongue
- James 4—Submit to God
- James 5—Power of Prayer

1. THE GIFT OF TRIALS
James 1:1-18

LEADER'S INSIGHT

The Bible is a remarkable book.

Some people have a crazy idea that the Bible isn't practical, that it makes little sense, and has no connection to real life today. Chances are they haven't read the Book of James. The first 18 verses deal with authentic life issues for both teens and adults: Facing hard times, handling temptations, what to do when one lacks wisdom, and how to overcome sin and addictions. Sounds like a reality TV show.

James understood hard times. He refers to them as "trials of many kinds." Trials come in many shapes and sizes. James not only deals with the difficulty they bring but also tells us that there's a benefit to trials. "Consider it a sheer gift, friends" James says (MSG). Trials are gifts that most people don't want, yet James tells us to "consider it pure joy" whenever we face trouble, suffering, and any kind of trial.

James defines a trial as "the testing of your faith" (verse 3). Why does our faith need to be tested? The same reason a teacher gives students an exam, to see if the knowledge is understood and applied. What happens to one's faith when life falls apart, a parent dies, or his or her best friend commits suicide? The testing of faith reveals what we really believe in and who we trust. Hard times show us what's deep inside our souls.

"The testing of your faith produces perseverance." Some versions use the word *endurance*, which literally means to "stand under." James is saying God's intent is to create resilience in our souls, the ability to "stand under" the worst possible test. He goes on to tell us that

"under pressure your faith life is forced into the open and shows its true colors" (verse 4 MSG). What color does the testing of your faith reveal? James tells us the intended outcome: "Let perseverance finish its work so that you may be mature and complete, not lacking anything" (verse 4).

The testing of our faith has a *purpose*. Trials are not meant to break us; they are used by God to mold us, to bring us into maturity and depth in our relationship with him. God's intent is our growth—and one of the tools God uses to help us dig deep is the testing of our faith.

James 1:1-18 helps us gain God's perspective on the tests of life and how to face temptations. In this session we learn how trials can be a gift from God.

Share
Warm-Up Questions

- What is one difficulty you faced as a kid?
- What are some ways people react to hard times?
- Why do people get irritated over the slightest trouble in life?

Observe
Observation Questions

- Read 1:1-8. What does this text say is the purpose of trials?
- Look at 1:9-11. What are some of the warnings listed here about money, wealth, and humility?
- Read verses 12-15. What does the writer say about temptations?
- In verses 16-18, what is James' message about God's character?

Think
Interpretation Questions

- Based on verses 1-8, why couldn't God use some other means to get our attention other than trials?

- Look at verses 8-10. Why do you think humility is important?

- Verses 11-15 say God does not test us to do evil. What does that mean?

- Read verses 16-18. Why does James speak about "every good and perfect gift"—and what does that have to do with the testing of our faith?

Apply

Application Questions

- How do you overcome and endure temptations and trials?

- What does it practically look like to be spiritually mature?

- How does our faith produce perseverance? Why does James connect handling trials with endurance? Is *endurance* the same as *perseverance*?

- What do you need to do in order to handle your own selfish and sinful desires?

Do

Optional Activity

Have your group collectively come up with as many trials as possible that both teenagers and adults face and list them on a piece of paper. Then determine as a group on a scale of 1 ("not a big deal") to 10 ("this is the worst trial") which are the most challenging hardships. Then have each student pick two of the trials that they've faced and how they handled them. Then pray as a group for strength and a deepening of one's faith.

QUIET TIME REFLECTIONS

Day 1: James 1:1-3

- What word or phrase jumps out to you? Why?

- Do you view yourself as a person of faith? Why or why not?

- Think about the phrase "when your faith is tested, your endurance has a chance to grow" (NLT) and what it means for your life. Is your endurance growing or not?

Day 2: James 1:4-6

- How does this passage speak to you?

- What advice is given to those who lack wisdom?

- Think about which temptations come your way. Where are you most vulnerable? Which temptations are the easiest to overcome? Difficult?

Day 3: James 1:7-9

- What insight do you gain from this text?

- What do you think about the idea that "doubt" is like the waves of the sea being tossed by the wind?

- Think about faith and doubt. Is it okay to doubt? Is it wrong? Can doubt be helpful in developing one's faith? How?

Day 4: James 1:10-12

- What's one question you have about this passage?

- What does it mean that the poor Christian should be glad and the rich shall be humbled? How does God honor the poor Christian?

- Think about how tests of our faith produce great character and endurance. Have you seen evidence of growth? If so, in what ways?

Day 5: James 1:13-14

- What can you learn from this text?

- Why does James say that God does not tempt us to do evil? What does that mean?

- Think about some ways you face temptation. Have you ever blamed God for the test? Why or why not?

Day 6: James 1:15-18

- What is God saying to you from these verses?

- How often do you thank God for the good gifts he's given you?

- Think about what it means to live "through the word of truth."

Day 7: James 1:1-18

Read through the entire passage. Write down the **one verse** that spoke to you the most this week. Commit the verse to memory for an extra challenge!

2. ORPHANS AND WIDOWS
James 1:19-27

LEADER'S INSIGHT

James' letter is a call to action.

Students need to understand that we are "saved" by faith, and that genuine faith leads to works. We are not saved by doing good works; rather we do good deeds *because* we are saved by God's grace. We don't do good in order to get to heaven; we do good works *because* we are going to heaven. James 1:19-27 can be summarized by three Rs—receive, remember, respond. God uses the Book of James to help us understand that the Christ-filled life is about living the truth.

- We *receive* God's Word. (verses 19-21)

- We *remember* God's Word. (22-25)

- We *respond* to God's Word. (26-27)

One of the most powerful passages in all of Scripture is James 1:19: "My dear brothers and sisters, always be willing to listen and slow to speak. Do not become angry easily." (New Century Version) As we receive the Word of God, we embrace the way of Jesus: quick to listen, slow to speak, do not become angry easily. Up until his last hours, after being tortured and beaten to a pulp, Jesus modeled James 1:19. He did not lash out verbally; instead, he stood humbly as he was tortured, hardly saying a word. I have a feeling that when James penned these words a decade after Jesus' ascension to heaven, he was thinking of how pain and hardship was demonstrated by his half-brother.

We *receive* the Word by understanding the words of James 1:20: "for the wrath of man does not produce the righteousness of God." (NKJV) Our anger doesn't help out God, nor does it make our lives look spiritually healthy. "God's righteousness doesn't grow from human anger." (MSG)

We *remember* God's Word. "And *remember*, it is a message to obey, not just to listen. For if you just listen and don't obey, it is like looking at your face in a mirror but doing nothing to improve your appearance." (verse 23 NLT) James is telling us that as we measure ourselves by the Word of God, it will give us perspective on who we really are, and that will lead us to freedom.

We *respond* in verses 26-27 to real human needs: The orphan and widow, two groups of people victimized through no fault of their own. Not only is "true religion" about taming our tongues (verse 26), but also we're called to take care of the least, those who are easily disregarded.

Share
Warm-Up Questions

- When you were a little kid, what was it like to sit and listen to someone talk for a long time?

- What are some good and bad ways to deal with anger?

- Why do people have a hard time listening well?

Observe
Observation Questions

- Read 1:19-22. What does this text say about our mouths and ears?

- Look at 23-24. What are some of the warnings listed here?

- Check out 25-26. What does the writer promise readers if they apply the truth?

- Read verses 27-28. What does James say about undefiled religion?

Think

Interpretation Questions

- Based on verses 19-20, why is the writer urging us to listen well?

- Look at verses 21-23. After hearing the Word, what are some reasons we don't do it?

- In verses 24-25, why is doing the Word compared with looking at a mirror?

- Read verses 26-27. Why do you think caring for widows and orphans is connected to true faith?

Apply

Application Questions

- Why is it hard to listen quickly and listen well?

- How does getting angry hurt your faith? Your friendships?

- What practical changes do you need to make to begin practicing what you are learning in the Word of God?

- What's one step you can take to care for orphans and widows?

Do

Optional Activity

Take your group to visit some of the elderly people from your church or an assisted living facility. Plan on asking great questions and listening well (James 1:19). Debrief your time and discover what each person learned from the experience of being with "shut ins" and widows/widowers.

QUIET TIME REFLECTIONS

Day 1: James 1:19

- What word or phrase jumps out to you? Why?

- Do you view yourself as one who is "quick to hear, slow to speak and slow to anger"? (NASB) Why or why not? Why are these traits important for a Christ-follower?

- Think about the phrase "slow to anger." What does this look like on a practical level? Are there things we *can* get angry about?

Day 2: James 1:20-21

- How does this passage speak to you?

- What attitudes are we to put aside as followers of Jesus? How's that working for you?

- Think about what it means to "humbly accept the word planted in you, which can save you." What can save us? Doesn't Jesus save us? Could James be talking about something deeper?

Day 3: James 1:22

- What insight do you gain from this text?

- What do you think about the idea that merely "listening" to the Word leads to deception? How is that possible?

- Think about why it's important for a Jesus-follower to "do" what the Word of God says.

Day 4: James 1:23-24

- What's one question you have about this passage?

- What is the connection between following God's Word and looking at oneself in the mirror? How often do you forget what you've just read?

- Think about how only *listening* to God's Word and not obeying it can hurt our witness and integrity.

Day 5: James 1:25-26

- What can you learn from this text?

- Why does James say that obedience leads to freedom? What kind of freedom?

- Think about one way you can apply God's Word today.

Day 6: James 1:27

- What is God saying to you from this verse?

- Why do you think James compares true religion with meeting the needs of orphans and widows?

- Think about what it means to "keep oneself from being polluted by the world." How is that even possible? What steps can you take today to make that happen?

Day 7: James 1:19-27

Read through the entire passage. Write down the **one verse** that spoke to you the most this week. Commit the verse to memory for an extra challenge!

3. DOES GOD PLAY FAVORITES?
James 2:1-13

LEADER'S INSIGHT

Why do we have favorites?

Most people would admit that they have favorites. They can tell you their favorite ice creams, favorite television shows, even their favorite pairs of shoes. What's more difficult to admit is that we actually play favorites when it comes to people. We often label others as more valuable or less valuable than us. We place a price tag on each person according to his or her talent, looks, socioeconomic status, family, skin color, and/or social standing.

James claims that there's no room for favoritism within the family of God. He makes the point that if you give someone dressed in fine clothing a special seat and direct the person dressed in rags to sit on the floor, you are a "judge with evil thoughts." (verse 4) James suggests that God can use anyone as long as that person is "rich in faith." (verse 5)

James' writings are born out of the great commandment that Jesus gives in Matthew 22:39—to love God and love others. James then ties back into Leviticus 19:15 which forbids anyone from showing favoritism to the rich or the poor. God's people cannot pick and choose what laws they will obey and what laws they will ignore because to "stumble at one point is to be guilty of breaking all of them." If someone in the church does everything by the letter of the law, yet gives priority to the rich over the poor, he or she has failed to live an obedient life.

The antidote to judgment is mercy. Be merciful to everyone, for when you extend mercy to others you will receive mercy in return. In this session, we learn how to extend mercy and refrain from playing favorites.

Share
Warm-Up Questions

- What was your favorite toy as a child?

- Why do you think people develop favorites in many areas of life?

- How can having favorites be a bad thing? Can it ever be good to have favorites?

Observe
Observation Questions

- Read 2:2-4. Why does James use this as an example to those he's writing to?

- Examine 2:5. Who has God chosen to inherit the Kingdom of God?

- According to 2:10, how many laws must be broken to be guilty of breaking them all?

- In 2:13, what does James say is better than judgment?

Think
Interpretation Questions

- What are the evil thoughts that James is referring to in 2:4? What makes them evil?

- Examine 2:5. What does James mean by someone being rich in faith?

- Why would breaking one of God's laws make you guilty of breaking them all? What is the outcome of breaking just one of God's laws?

- How does someone show judgment without mercy?

Apply

Application Questions

- What is your equivalent of the church's meetings referred to in 2:2?

- Who in your culture or community are favored and who are disgraced?

- How can you rethink the severity of the laws that we break each and every day?

- What is one practical way to keep you from showing favoritism toward people this week?

Do

Optional Activity

As an individual or a group, commit to serving in a location where those who are usually marginalized are present. It could be a soup kitchen, orphanage, or homeless shelter. Before going to serve, pray for God to give you the eyes of Christ to be able to value each person the same. Afterward debrief your time and mention one person you met by name and then pray for that person.

QUIET TIME REFLECTIONS

Day 1: James 2:1-4

- What word or phrase jumps out to you? Why?

- Why does James refer to the reader as a "brother" or "sister"? How does that enhance his point in this verse?

- Try to go through today and not judge people based on outward appearances.

Day 2: James 2:5

- How does this passage speak to you?

- How can someone be "poor in the eyes of the world" yet "rich in faith"?

- How will people be treated in that Kingdom based on this passage?

Day 3: James 2:6-7

- What insight do you gain from this text?

- What point is James making when he points out to readers that they have exploited the poor for the favor of the rich— and yet the rich are the very ones who are taking them to court and mistreating them? What good is it to show favor toward someone who will do you wrong?

- Are there people in your life that you "butter up" or "give favor to" who turn around and disgrace Jesus Christ? Is it worth it?

Day 4: James 2:8-10

- What's one question you have about this passage?

- How would you grade yourself on loving your neighbor as yourself? How would God grade you on a scale of A to F?

- Which of God's laws do you still find difficult to abide by? What's one way you can practice obedience in these areas?

Day 5: James 2:11

- What can you learn from this text?

- Why do you think God gave the Israelites the Ten Commandments? Are they still pertinent today?

- How does being a lawbreaker make you feel? In what way does this reveal the need for Jesus to go to the cross?

Day 6: James 2:12-13

- What is God saying to you from these verses?

- Why is it so hard to have mercy on people?

- Can you recall a time where God had mercy on you? How did you respond?

Day 7: James 2:1-13

Read through the entire passage. Write down the **one verse** that spoke to you the most this week. Commit the verse to memory for an extra challenge!

4. FAITH AND WORKS
James 2:14-24

LEADER'S INSIGHT

Social justice is hip and cool these days.

We see organizations that sponsor orphans around the world to end hunger. We see movements to end the abduction of child soldiers. We see massive movements to end slavery even in the United States. If you can think of a good cause, there is probably an organization for it. But how important are works if we're not made right with God through faith?

In these 10 verses, James explains not only how our good works should be evident in our lives, but also how necessary they are to our faith. James explains in this passage that faith and works are both part of the equation. Verse 17 actually says that faith without works is dead. If we truly believe what we say, we will in fact act upon it. It is a matter of having a faith so strong and so radical that we cannot help but do something about it. James goes on to give us the Old Testament example of Abraham. In speaking about Abraham in verse 22 James says, "You see his faith and his actions were working together, and his faith was made complete by his actions." Faith and actions are both part of being a God-follower. Our faith is not complete until we do it. We cannot truly say we have faith until we actually take the leap.

It's all well and good that teens state they believe in Christ, but until one moves into a place of action, faith is not truly complete. As James says, it's dead. We need to challenge teens to move past a shallow faith to a place of action. When they reach that point of radical faith, they truly have the power to make a difference for the kingdom of heaven. In this session we learn just how important our actions are in our daily Christian walk.

Share

Warm-Up Questions

- Do you think actions speak louder than words?

- What do you think of people who say one thing and do another?

- What are some examples of good deeds?

Observe

Observation Questions

- Read 2:14-17. How important does the text say good deeds are to faith?

- Look at verses 18-19. Why is belief simply not enough according to these verses?

- Verses 20-22 give us the Old Testament example of Abraham. How does this text explain the relationship of good deeds and faith?

- How was Abraham made a friend of God, according to verses 23-24?

Think

Interpretation Questions

- After looking at verses 14-17, why is it useless to merely claim or say something?

- Based on 18-19, why are our actions the evidence of what we believe?

- Look at 20-22. Why are actions necessary for completing our faith?

- In verses 23-24 James says a person is justified by his actions as well as his faith. What does *justified* mean and how do actions play a role in that?

Apply

- Have you ever thought about solving some problem but never did anything? If so, when?

- Would you consider the average Christian to have a "complete faith"? Why/why not?

- Is it possible to have a healthy faith without good deeds? Why or why not?

- Judging by your actions, would your faith be considered alive or dead? What is one step you could take to make your faith more alive?

Do

Optional Activity

Have each of your group members write down two or three actions they could take to improve their family, school, or church. Then go around as a group and discuss how improvements can be made. Finally take turns praying for the person next to you to make an impact.

QUIET TIME REFLECTIONS

Day 1: James 2:14

- What word or phrase jumps out to you? Why?

- Would you say you have more faith or deeds?

- Do you think that faith without deeds can save you? Why or why not?

Day 2: James 2:15-16

- How does this passage speak to you?

- How does James illustrate the importance of deeds?

- Have you ever seen someone who needed clothes or food? What did you do?

Day 3: James 2:17

- What insight do you gain from this text?

- Why would faith be dead if not accompanied by action? Do your actions prove your faith?

- How often do you act on what you believe?

Day 4: James 2:18-19

- What is one question you have about this passage?

- Why do you think our faith needs to move past simply believing in God?

- What does it mean to "believe" in God?

Day 5: James 2:20-22

- What can you learn from this text?

- Read Genesis 22:1-11. How does Abraham's faith connect with your life of faith?

- Why do actions make faith complete? How do they work together?

Day 6: James 2:23-24

- What is God saying to you from these verses?

- Would you be considered a friend of God like Abraham?

- What does *justified* mean? How are we justified through works as well as faith?

Day 7: James 2:14-24

Read through the entire passage. Write down the **one verse** that spoke to you the most this week. Commit the verse to memory for an extra challenge!

5. WORDS WILL NEVER HURT YOU?
James 3:1-12

LEADER'S INSIGHT

Words matter.

One measure of our spiritual maturity and growth as a Jesus-follower has to do with the words we speak. In this section, James talks candidly about taming the tongue. It's hard to believe that what we say has so much power to affect others. When James wrote his letter almost 2,000 years ago, words were mainly expressed in person or in the occasional written letter. Since not everyone could read, speaking was the most common form of communication.

Today the words that come out of our mouths and the words that come from our fingertips in the form of Twitter, Facebook, and texts can spread rapidly to large groups of people. The fact that our words can be a blessing or a curse still holds true today, but the damage can be even farther reaching because of the impact that social media has on communication.

Not only does James emphasize the content of our speech, but he also addresses the source of our words (verses 11-12). It is interesting to note that Scripture mentions the connection between the condition of our hearts and the words we speak. Matthew 12:34 reads, "For the mouth speaks what the heart is full of." What a powerful reminder to constantly evaluate the condition of our hearts—which is the source of our words.

In this session, students will learn that even though our tongues are small, they can give life or death, encouragement or destruction, to those around us.

Share

- Share something you think is small that has a large impact.

- How have your words gotten you in trouble? Give one example.

- How do you feel when people speak negatively about you? How do you feel when people give you positive comments?

Observe

Observation Questions

- We know that our "actions" matter to God. James begins the first two verses in chapter 3 stating the importance of what?

- Read 3:3-5. James compares the tongue to what other objects? What are the similarities between the objects?

- Look at verses 7-8. Explain how the word *tamed* is used in discussing the human tongue.

- Verses 9-10 share the positive and negative abilities of the tongue—what are they?

Think

Interpretation Questions

- Read verse 2. Is it possible to "never be at fault" in what we say? Why or why not?

- Look at 3:8. What do you think James means when he writes, "no human being can tame the tongue"?

- Reflect on verses 9-10. How can both praises and curses come from the same source (i.e., person)?

- Read verses 11-12. How do the examples of a spring, a fig tree, and a grapevine all relate to the words we speak?

Apply
Application Questions

- What are some of the reasons people say negative things, curse, or gossip? Do you do these things to others?

- How have your words in the past week hurt your friends or family?

- How can you repair the damage you have caused by your words?

- What's one step you could take to make sure the words are blessings and not curses?

Do
Optional Activity

Have each person in your group write his or her name on the top of a sheet of paper and pass it to the person next to him or her. Instruct everybody to write a blessing (something appreciated about the person named at the top of the paper). Keep passing the papers until each person has his or her paper back. Tell everyone to read silently the comments on their papers. Ask the group to share how the comments made them feel. Discuss what practical ways they can "speak a blessing" to others this coming week. Ask them to share the results next week.

QUIET TIME REFLECTIONS

Day 1: James 3:1-2

- What word or phrase jumps out to you? Why?

- Why are teachers singled out in this chapter regarding "taming the tongue," and why do you think they "will be judged more strictly"?

- Read verse 2. Do you think it's possible for someone to speak only positive things? Why or why not?

Day 2: James 3:3-4

- How does this passage speak to you?

- Why does James use the examples of the horse's bit and the ship's rudder to describe the human tongue?

- Think about ways your small tongue has caused large problems.

Day 3: James 3:5-6

- What insight do you gain from this text?

- Why does James compare the tongue to a fire and the damage it can cause?

- Think about how your words are like a fire. Have you ever started any "fires"? Are there any "fires" you need to put out?

Day 4: James 3:7-8

- What's one question you have about this passage?

- What is possible to tame and what is impossible to tame?

- Think about the ways your tongue is "evil, full of deadly poison." Do you need to ask God for forgiveness for any words you have used this week?

Day 5: James 3:9-10

- What can you learn from this text?

- What affects the content of what you communicate to others?

- Think about ways you can praise God more and say fewer negative things to and about others.

Day 6: James 3:11-12

- What is God saying to you from these verses?

- What does the choice of words spoken say about the person who's speaking?

- Think about what steps you can take to guard your mouth.

Day 7: James 3:1-12

Read through the entire passage. Write down the **one verse** that spoke to you the most this week. Commit the verse to memory for an extra challenge!

6. TWO TYPES OF WISDOM
James 3:13-18

LEADER'S INSIGHT

Intelligence and wisdom are characteristics often sought out but difficult to attain.

What student wouldn't want to be smarter or wiser? James 3:13-18 looks at the concept of wisdom, asking the reader "do you want to be counted wise, to build a reputation for wisdom?" (verse 13 MSG) Most would say yes, but James will walk us through two types of wisdom, and what God says is required for real wisdom.

James states, "It's the way you live, not the way you talk that counts." (MSG) Then James proceeds to tell us what *not* to do. In verses 14-16 he writes, "Mean spirited ambition isn't wisdom. Boasting that you are wise isn't wisdom. Twisting the truth to make you sound wise isn't wisdom." James goes on to say that it's so far from what wisdom is that it's in fact *demonic.* How many of us have experienced the troubles that come with climbing the ladder of success? It's exactly what James describes in verse 16 "whenever you're trying to look better than others or get the better of them, things fall apart and everyone ends up at each other's throats." (MSG)

So how do you live wisely? Verse 17 tells us that we grow in wisdom by responding gently and reasonably, treating others with respect and giving others the honor they deserve as a child of God. James tells us that others will see this wisdom "if you do the hard work of getting along with each other." In other words, living out God's wisdom isn't an easy road, but if diligently followed, it will yield great rewards and true godly knowledge.

Share

Warm-Up Questions

- Who in your life do you consider wise? Why?

- Name some things in your life that keep you from growing in wisdom?

- Do you think people in our culture today value wisdom? Why/why not?

Observe

Observation Questions

- Read verses 13-14. What does James say to do and not do in order to live wisely?

- Look at verse 15. Where do the two types of wisdom come from?

- What does verse 16 say happens when we treat others poorly?

- In verses 17-18, how is godly wisdom compared to earthly wisdom?

Think

Interpretation Questions

- Look at verses 13-14. Why do you think humility is a crucial part of living wisely?

- In verse 15, why do you think James states that wisdom can be demonic?

- Read verse 16 and examine the connection between disorder and selfish ambition. What does that look like?

- Look at verses 17-18. Why do you think James speaks about peacemakers, and what needs to be sowed in order to reap a righteous harvest?

Apply

- How do we determine who is wise and who to surround ourselves with?

- What can you do to overcome bitterness and envy toward others? Who could help you in this process?

- What brings disorder (or chaos) to your life? How do you try to manage it? What part of this passage could help you?

- What for you is the hardest area in which to show mercy and grace? How have you tried to show those qualities to others? How could you show those qualities to others?

Do

Optional Activity

Have the students come up with a list of what godly wisdom looks like in contrast to earthly wisdom. Have them determine as a group which wisdom they tend to display and have them talk about two to three ways they can keep encouraging each other to grow in godly wisdom. Then pray as a group for strength in living a life of humility and growing in wisdom.

QUIET TIME REFLECTIONS

Day 1: James 3:13

- What word or phrase jumps out to you? Why?

- Do you view yourself as someone who does good deeds? Why or why not?

- Think about the term *humility*. How are deeds done in humility different than just good deeds?

Day 2: James 3:14

- How does this passage speak to you?

- What bitterness is still present in your life? Why is it hard to let it go?

- Think about the selfishness in your heart. Why is it tough to focus on others rather than yourself?

Day 3: James 3:15

- What insight do you gain from this text?

- Do people in the world today ever think being jealous and selfish is wise? What would James say about that? How do we discern godly wisdom from worldly wisdom?

- Think about how you fall into seeking unspiritual wisdom? Is it easy to fall into that? Is it working?

Day 4: James 3:16

- What's one question you have about this passage?

- Think about chaos in your life. Where do you think it comes from? What does James say about it?

- What causes a person to envy? What causes you to have envy? How do you deal with it?

Day 5: James 3:17

- What can you learn from this text?

- Think about wisdom from heaven. Is heavenly wisdom easy to attain? How does it differ from earthly wisdom?

- Reflect on the terms *pure and sincere*. Why do you think heavenly wisdom calls for these qualities? How can you work toward being pure and sincere?

Day 6: James 3:18

- What is God saying to you from this verse?

- Reflect on the term *peacekeeper*. What is a peacekeeper? Why does being a peacekeeper require godly wisdom?

- Sowing and reaping are activities related to farming. What do you think it means to "sow" peace in your daily life? What does James suggest you will reap if you don't sow peace?

Day 7: James 3:13-18

Read through the entire passage. Write down the **one verse** that spoke to you the most this week. Commit the verse to memory for an extra challenge!

7. THE CAUSE OF CONFLICTS
James 4:1-12

LEADER'S INSIGHTS

James lays out a great argument of selfish ambition versus humility.

If we're looking for a passage in the Bible that deals with the condition of the human heart, this is the one. It sheds light on who we are, who God is, and how—as followers of Christ—we should treat others.

James says, "Where jealousy and selfish ambition exist, there will be disorder and every vile practice." (3:16 ESV) In chapter 4 he is talking precisely about that; that our selfish ambitions cause us to fight and quarrel.

We have to get what we *want*, or we are not "happy." And if we aren't happy people, the people around us won't be, either. This is a problem with our inner persons. It's a heart problem, which is consumed with pride. I desire power and authority; I want material things. I will go out of my way to get these things. "What causes you to fight and quarrel?" James asks. "Is it not because your passions are at war within you?" Our sinful passions are clearly evident in our lives.

James says that when Christians desire things above God, we disdain the grace he's shown to us on the cross and resurrection. That's a sobering message. What's more amazing is the fact that James tells us that in spite of this, "He gives more grace." (verse 6) Wow.

God continuously gives us grace even though we oppose or ignore him. This session challenges us about our sinful nature and our selfish ambition. Receiving God's grace and walking in humility is the remedy.

Share

- Share about a time when you fought to get something you wanted.

- How do you usually handle a fight?

- Why is it hard to be humble? In what ways do you tend to judge your neighbors (i.e., your friends, fellow students, family, etc.)?

Observe

Observation Questions

- Read 4:1-4. What is the cause of all of our fights and quarrels?

- Look at 4:6-10. Compare and contrast the things James is saying. Make a pros and cons chart on Humility Versus Pride based on these verses.

- Look at verses 11-12. What do they say about judging our brothers and sisters?

Think

Interpretation Questions

- Look at verses 1-4. Why is friendship with the world tantamount to enmity with God?

- Read verse 5. Why do you think God is jealous about us? What does that mean?

- Verses 6-10. Why does God want us to be humble? Why is it important?

- Read verses 11-12. What does it mean that one shouldn't be a judge of the Law?

Apply

Application Questions

- What are some practical steps you can take to overcome your sinful desires?

- How might serving other people help you grow in humility?

- Why do you tend to judge others? What can you do to change this?

Do

Optional Activity

Have each group member write down two ways in which he or she recently chose to be selfish or prideful—then an example of the opposite of each selfish demonstration. Have them separate into smaller groups if applicable and pray for those things to be imparted to them. Also pray through verses 7-10 and that God will give them grace for greater change.

QUIET TIME REFLECTIONS

Day 1: James 4:1-3

- What word or phrase jumps out to you? Why?

- What kind of fights and quarrels do you think James is thinking about? Why do we have these evil passions in us? Where do they come from?

- How can we ask rightly as opposed to wrongly? What kinds of things should we ask for?

Day 2: James 4:4-5

- How does this passage speak to you?

- Make a list of "friendship of the world" and "friendship with God." Why are those things either in alignment with God or against God? Can you use Scripture to back up your findings?

- Contemplate what James means by "He yearns jealously over the spirit that he has made to dwell in us."

Day 3: James 4:6

- What insight do you gain from this text?

- What does it mean to be proud? Humble? How can we take steps to become more humble?

- Contemplate ways you've been proud or humble lately. Pray for grace over these things.

DAY 4: James 4:7-8

- What's one question you have about this passage?

- How do we submit to God? What does that look like? If knowing the promise of drawing near to God gives us victory over temptation, how will you change?

- What do you think James means when he says, "Cleanse your hands, you sinners, and purify your hearts, you double-minded"?

Day 5: James 4:9-10

- What can you learn from this text?

- How should we treat our sin in light of these verses?

- How do you think the Lord will exalt you if you are humble?

Day 6: James 4:11-12

- What is God saying to you in these verses?

- What do you think it means to "judge your neighbor"? What do you think it means if you "judge the law; you are not a doer of the law but a judge"?

- Contemplate ways you can be less judgmental toward others.

Day 7: James 4:1-12

Read through the entire passage. Write down the **one verse** that spoke to you the most this week. Commit the verse to memory for an extra challenge!

8. GOD'S WILL AND THE FUTURE
James 4:13-17

LEADER'S INSIGHT

If you're a follower of Jesus, live like it.

That's James' message. His book focuses on this one primary passion. The brother of Jesus is concerned that God's people, dispersed among the non-Christians of the world, have begun to lose their hearts for Christ-like living. They are supposed to live unpolluted by the world (James 1:27). That's what this passage addresses. How does one live in a world where every day you make decisions that don't seem to involve God, decisions that don't seem to *need* God's involvement?

As good stewards of our time and work we need to think through the details of life, whether we're picking our classes for next semester, applying for a particular job, or thinking about an item we'd like to buy. What can be wrong with that?

Only this: James wants us to remember that life is temporary (a "mist" in verse 14), and we should be prepared for the unexpected ("you do not even know what will happen tomorrow" verse 14). The big deal is that God has been left out of the picture. That's the point of verse 15. God is in control of the universe, and he continues to be in charge even though many people ignore him daily. Those who've not submitted to Christ are expected to ignore God, but not his own people!

Those who say, "If the Lord wills" (verse 15) have considered God's plan prior to their next steps, regardless of the situation. They have taken into account their faith in Christ. They are acknowledging him in all their ways, trusting that he will make their paths straight. (Proverbs 3:5-6)

Verse 17 notes the "sin of omission." It's bad enough when we do things that God has clearly told us not to do. How much worse is it if we also ignore the good things we *are* supposed to do? Not only do we need to be aware of what we are *not* supposed to do—we also need to be aware of what we *are* supposed to do.

And what are we supposed to do? James tells us to bring every area of our lives—no matter how seemingly mundane or unworthy of God's attention—under the direction of his will. This is true even if we feel like we already know what we should do. We're to pray about all things (Philippians 4:6) and give every detail of our family lives, school, sports, youth group, and friendships up to Jesus. At the very least we must recognize that our best plans are subject to God's leading or even last-minute reorganization. In fact, it's the way we're supposed to live.

SHARE

WARM-UP QUESTIONS

- What do you plan to do after you graduate?

- What's your dream job?

- What do you do in a situation if you don't know what you're *supposed* to do?

Observe

Observation Questions

- Read verses 13-14. What's James trying to remind these people?

- Look at verse 15. What point is James trying to make?

- What is the connection between verse 16 and verse 13?

- How does verse 17 describe a "sin of omission"?

Think

- Look at verses 13-14. What have these people failed to take into account?

- Read verse 15. If God is sovereign and in control of all things, why do you think it's important for us to acknowledge him in what we do?

- In verse 16, why is James accusing these people of boasting? Do you think they thought they were boasting?

- Read verse 17. What error in this specific situation led to sin?

Apply

Application Questions

- What plans have you been making without asking for God's input or direction?

- James teaches that life is a "mist" or "vapor." If you're only alive for a limited time, how should this impact the way you live?

- Describe how a student or businessperson is just as much in need of God's direction as a pastor or missionary. How can you start to live with God's direction?

- Is there an area in your life in which you know you're supposed to do something, but you've been resisting God's will?

Do

Optional Activity

Take time in your group to discuss areas in which it's common for Christian students NOT to seek God's will, input, or direction. Write a list of these areas. Then take each area and discuss the potential difference in outcomes between living that area in one's own strength versus seeking God's will. Pray for God to give you his wisdom for daily living in ALL areas.

QUIET TIME REFLECTIONS

Day 1: James 4:13-14

- What word or phrase jumps out to you? Why?

- Have you been making any plans where you have not prayed for God's wisdom and leadership? Think about how your life will turn out if you live depending only on your own strength and wisdom.

- Think about a time in your life where things didn't turn out like you'd planned. What does that teach you about your capacity to control your destiny?

Day 2: James 4:14

- How does this passage speak to you?

- James calls our lives a mist or vapor. How does that make you feel? Does it affect the way you want to live the rest of your life?

- The shortness of life may make some people feel uncomfortable or sad. However, others may view this as an opportunity to make positive changes. What are some positive changes you can make in your life?

Day 3: James 4:15

- What insight do you gain from this text?

- What are ways you can seek God's will for your life? Is God's will always crystal clear? When God's will doesn't seem clear, how can you use the words of this verse in your circumstance?

- Is there a person you know who seems to live for God consistently? What is it about that person's life that inspires you? What's one aspect of his or her faith that you can incorporate into your own life?

Day 4: James 4:16

- What's one question you have about this passage?

- Consider areas in your life where you might be guilty of "boasting or bragging" (NIV). How might God want to grow you in your faith in spite of you falling short in this area?

- Pride and arrogance are normal struggles, even for Christians. Think about areas in which you've been too proud to submit to God.

Day 5: James 4:13 & 16

- What can you learn from this text?

- Consider how these two verses are connected. Do you think these people realize they're boasting? Are there areas in your life in which you might be guilty of boasting, but not realize it?

- When we realize we've been sinning, how should we respond?

Day 6: James 4:17

- What is God saying to you from this verse?

- Read this verse several times. Consider how it can be applied to those described in verse 13. How can this verse be applied to your life in general?

- The people mentioned in this verse didn't likely consider their actions sinful. Consider how James would coach them to live differently. How might James coach you to live differently?

Day 7: James 4:13-17

Read through the entire passage. Write down the **one verse** that spoke to you the most this week. Commit the verse to memory for an extra challenge!

9. HANDLING MONEY
James 5:1-12

LEADER'S INSIGHT

We live in a dog-eat-dog world.

Much of it's about how much we get for ourselves. We also live on a technology-crazed planet where it's all about getting the next new thing faster than anybody else. Malcolm Forbes is famous for his quote: "He who dies with the most toys wins." Sadly this is reflective of our culture—the false notion that the end goal is to get the most stuff.

James says quite the opposite. This chapter starts with a warning: "Now listen, you rich people, weep and wail because of the misery coming upon you." All the wealth we still have with us when we die will be evidence for how selfish we were—and how little we cared about others. There's nothing wrong with making money—what matters is what you do with it. Keeping it for yourself and spending it selfishly will bring judgment.

Judgment also comes when the rich take advantage of the poor. When we take advantage of those underneath or less fortunate than us in order to get ahead, we bring further condemnation upon ourselves.

So what are those who don't have anything supposed to do? In verses 7-12, James addresses the poor and those who are being taken advantage of. He writes that the poor and oppressed should be patient and stand firm to be an example to those around them. He warns the poor not to grumble against each other—or even grumble against those who are oppressing them.

Whether you are rich or poor, God is interested in the condition of your heart. If you have money and possessions, what you do with them shows the condition of your hearts. If you don't have anything, whether you persevere or grumble through your earthly struggle shows the condition of your heart.

In this session, you'll learn that how we treat money and people is a reflection of who we are—and whose we are.

Share
Warm-Up Questions

- What is your most important possession?

- Do you think money is important? Why or why not?

- Would you consider yourself to have a lot of patience? Why/why not?

Observe
Observation Questions

- Read 5:1-3. What does the text say will happen to wealth when Jesus comes back?

- Look at verses 4-6. How have rich people gained their wealth?

- Read verses 7-9. What's the right response to suffering? What's the wrong response?

- What are some examples of perseverance based on verses 10-12?

Think
Interpretation Questions

- Looking at verses 5:1-3, why would hoarded wealth testify against us?

- In verses 5:4-6, why does James refer to getting "fat"?

- Read verses 5:7-9. What do you think our reward will be for being patient?

- Why do you suppose James mentions swearing oaths and being true to your word in verses 5:10-12?

Apply

Application Questions

- Do you hoard your money and possessions? What's the danger of putting our trust in earthly possessions and riches? Where should we place our trust?

- Have you ever oppressed anyone or mistreated anyone? Who do you need to stop mistreating?

- When you are mistreated or oppressed, do you tend to react with patience or grumbling? What do you think is happening in your heart when you grumble?

- Have you ever sworn an oath? Do you think others can trust your word? If not, what's one step you can take toward becoming more trustworthy in regard to your words?

Do

Optional Activity

Have each student take out their cell phones, wallets, and anything else on their persons. Put all of it in the middle of the floor. If it takes around $1 a day to feed someone in an impoverished area in the world, figure out how many people you could feed with the pile of stuff in the middle. Then give that amount of money to the local homeless shelter or food pantry.

QUIET TIME REFLECTIONS

Day 1: James 5:1-2

- What word or phrase jumps out to you? Why?

- What misery is coming for rich people?

- Think about a time when you cried or wailed. Why did you?

Day 2: James 5:3-4

- How does this passage speak to you?

- Why would hoarding riches count against you? Do you think that your money and stuff would testify for you or against you?

- Think about why culture is so consumed by stuff. What do you rely on to satisfy your heart?

Day 3: James 5:5

- What insight do you gain from this text?

- Do you live in luxury and self-indulgence? How about compared to the rest of the world?

- Think about possessions. How do they make you "fat" in the sense James is referring to here?

Day 4: James 5:6-7

- What's one question you have about this passage?

- What should those who follow Jesus do as they wait for his return? What does this look like, practically, as you live each day?

- Think about a farmer planting crops. Why is that like a Christian waiting for Jesus' return?

Day 5: James 5:8-9

- What can you learn from this text?

- Where do you need to be patient and stand firm right now?

- Think about the phrase "The Judge is standing at the door." What does it mean? How often do you judge others?

Day 6: James 5:10-12

- What is God saying to you through these verses?

- Try to name some Old Testament prophets. Why are the prophets good examples of perseverance?

- Think about the phrase, "Let your Yes be yes, and your No, no." What is meant by this phrase? Could you count this true for you?

Day 7: James 5:1-12

Read through the entire passage. Write down the **one verse** that spoke to you the most this week. Commit the verse to memory for an extra challenge!

10. HUMAN LIKE ELIJAH
James 5:13-20

LEADER'S INSIGHT

The Bible is like a rare jewel.

We tend to read the Scriptures and say, "That was nice," and then move on to other things. If you can encourage students to take the time to really analyze and ponder some verses, the Bible will come alive. James 5:13-20 is one of those rare jewels.

Based on how much praying James must have done, you could say his nickname was "Camel Knees." Evidently James spent extended time praying — so, as Chuck Swindoll has said, his knees became calloused. It's not surprising for James to mention prayer in his writings. The Book of James contains 108 verses, and 54 verses are commands. "Is anyone in trouble? He should pray." (verse 13) How fitting that our final session on James begins with a call to prayer.

Teens understand that life is hard and James does not shy away from the topic of suffering. When we face hard times, James says to pray. When people are sick, we're to call for the leaders of the church "to pray over them and anoint them with oil in the name of the Lord." (5:14)

But prayer is more than just a checklist of asking God for favors. It's not just an extinguisher to put fires out. Prayer in the Bible is also about praising God, worshiping God in song, being silent, listening to God, and confessing sins. James uses a famous prophet in the book of Kings—Elijah—to illustrate the power of prayer.

Like Elijah, we too can see our prayers become realities. "Elijah was a man just like us. He prayed earnestly that it would not rain, and it did not rain on the land for three and a half years. Again he prayed, and the heavens gave rain, and the earth produced its crops." (5:17-18)

And we, like Elijah, need to know *what* to pray for (God's will) and *when* to pray for it (God's timing). Sometimes we wonder, "Why pray if God already knows the outcome?" Students need to understand that prayer does more for us than for God. Of course God is delighted when we talk with him, but the truth of the matter is that prayer deepens *our* intimacy with God. The object of prayer is not getting the answer *yes;* rather it's simply *God.* Connecting and relating with the almighty God—and developing that relationship—is the goal. James challenges us to pray when we are sick, when things are tough—and when life is good. Simply put: Pray!

James finishes up his fifth and final chapter with a seemingly strange and abrupt conclusion. He speaks of those who once walked with God and started to walk away. It's stated clearly in *The Message:* "My dear friends, if you know people who have wandered off from God's truth, don't write them off. Go after them. Get them back and you will have rescued precious lives from destruction and prevented an epidemic of wandering away from God."

Who do you know who's walked away from God? Make an intentional decision to help that person make a 180-degree turn back to God. James tells us that chances *are slim that* the wanderer will return (i.e., repent) without some type of personal connection. That might mean getting in someone's face and using tough love. Sometimes it requires a more gentle approach (Galatians 6:1).

Either way, "go after them."

James' book begins and ends with a challenge for us to do good works. Remember this from James: *True faith produces an authentic lifestyle of good deeds.*

Share

Warm-Up Questions

- Name a difficult time you've faced that caused you to pray.

- Why do you think prayer is hard? Is it ever easy? If so, when?

- What family member or friend needs prayer today?

Observe

Observation Questions

- See verses 13-14. What should a sick person do?

- What is the promised result of prayer for the sick noted in verses 15-16?

- What example does James give to illustrate effective, powerful prayer? (verses 16-18)

- How does James conclude his book? (verses 19-20)

Think

Interpretation Questions

- Why do you think prayer for healing seldom seems to happen?

- Is there a connection between sinning and sickness?

- Why do you think some people are healed and others are not?

- Do we trust too much in doctors and medicine to the exclusion of God?

Apply

Application Questions

- How can you grow more deeply in your prayer life?

- What's one prayer request you have that literally only God can pull off?

- Who has modeled an amazing prayer life to you? Why not ask that person to teach you more about prayer?

- Is there a friend who has spiritually drifted whom you need to bring back into the fold?

Do

Optional Activity

Take on this initiative game: MISSING IN ACTION (MIA). Have students come up with a list of friends whom they think could be "taking a break from God." Maybe they have stopped coming to small group, youth group, or church? Have your students make an effort to reach out to those friends and encourage your students to be intentional about inviting them back.

Warning: Don't assume that absence from Christian events means that students have walked away from God. Another bad assumption is the opposite: That those who attend everything are doing great in their relationships with Jesus. Youth group and church attendance is just one sign of where a person's heart is. There's no doubt that kids in your group know who's dropped out. But be sure to put yourself in the place of the teen who's gone MIA. Maybe he's mad at God, maybe she's been sick, or perhaps he feels the youth group doesn't even care he's gone. And there could be a lot of other reasons for their absences: Maybe there's been a family crisis or maybe they play year-round soccer. Reach out in love and concern, above all.

QUIET TIME REFLECTIONS

Day 1: James 5:13

- What word or phrase jumps out to you? Why?
- What kind of suffering warrants prayer? What types of suffering have you experienced?
- What has happened in the last 24 hours that's made you happy, something you are thankful for? Take a few moments to thank God for this.

Day 2: James 5:14

- How does this passage speak to you?
- What's the importance of calling leaders to pray for us when we're sick? What's wrong with praying individually?
- What would it take for you to call for help from others if you get sick or are struggling with something?

Day 3: James 5:15

- What insight do you gain from this text?
- Have you ever wondered if sin leads to sickness?
- Who do you know who's sick? It says that the "prayer offered in faith will restore the one who is sick." Could you be the person God uses to help the sick person through him?

Day 4: James 5:16

- What is one question you have about this passage?
- What sins do you need to confess today?
- What does it look like for you to become "effective" in your prayers?

Day 5: James 5:17-18

- What can you learn from this text?

- In what ways are you like (or different than) the prophet Elijah? How does reading about his prayer help you become more courageous in your faith?

- What powerful prayer do you need to pray that could change someone's life?

Day 6: James 5:19-20

- What is God saying to you through these verses?

- What does it look like for someone to wander away from the faith? How does this happen?

- Think about one friend who's wandering from the faith? What would it take for you to go after that person?

Day 7: James 5:13-20

Read through the entire passage. Write down the **one verse** that spoke to you the most this week. Commit the verse to memory for an extra challenge!

Part 2

The Letters of First and Second Peter

HANDY INSIGHTS AND TIPS ON FIRST AND SECOND PETER

WHO? Peter was raised in a Jewish family and was a fisherman by trade, chosen by Jesus to be one of his first disciples (Jesus selected 12 disciples/apostles). Peter was a zealous and impetuous man, what we might call an external processer. Some say he had "foot in the mouth disease." Peter had many ups and downs in his life. He promised Jesus that he would never deny him, but he denied Jesus three times—and in the hour of Christ's greatest need. Peter walked away deeply broken and ashamed. But after Jesus rose again, he restored Peter. Later Peter became filled with the Holy Spirit with other disciples on the Day of Pentecost and became one of the boldest leaders in the early church. Jesus told Peter that he would build the church upon him and his leadership (Matthew 16:18) and the gates of hell would not prevail.

Peter wrote these two letters to empower and encourage the people of God to keep growing in their faith no matter how tough the times they were living in.

WHERE? Peter is writing to "God's elect, exiles scattered," rendered in the Holman Christian Standard Bible translation as "temporary residents of the Dispersion." The NASB reads, "to those who reside as aliens." The term *dispersion* (i.e., *diasporas* in the Greek) typically refers to the Jewish people scattered throughout the five different regions of Asia Minor—and for this reason some are convinced that the letters' primary readers were Jewish believers in Jesus (*Yeshua* is the Hebrew name for Jesus). The book of 1 Peter was written toward the end of his life and 2 Peter just prior to his death. Tradition indicates Peter was crucified upside down.

WHEN? Some believe the letters of 1 and 2 Peter were written around A.D. 65-68. In July of A.D. 64, a great fire broke out in Rome that destroyed numerous buildings and left many of its citizens homeless. When suspicion fell on the Emperor Nero, he diverted the rage of the people by placing blame on Christians. Peter is writing primarily to Jewish believers in Jesus and a number of Gentile Christians facing suffering and persecution.

WHAT? After Jesus' death, resurrection, and ascension, the early church experienced dramatic and amazing numerical and spiritual growth. One of the ways of communicating truth to Jewish and Gentile Christians in the midst of persecution was through writing letters to the local churches (or assemblies).

Peter wrote two letters (1 and 2 Peter). He identifies himself as the author of 1 Peter (1:1) and 2 Peter (again 1:1) and states that he writes from Babylon (5:13)—most likely another name for Rome.

Words to Remember in 1 Peter:

- Chapter 1—*Hope*
- Chapter 2—*Honor*
- Chapter 3—*Harmony*
- Chapter 4—*Healthy*
- Chapter 5—*Humility*

2 Peter Themes:

- Chapter 1—Faith
- Chapter 2—Judgment
- Chapter 3—Day of the Lord

11. A LIVING HOPE
1 Peter 1:1-12

LEADER'S INSIGHT

Peter was an outspoken follower of Jesus.

He wrote to an audience of Christ-followers in order to help them understand the new life they had in Christ. Peter refers to himself as "an apostle on assignment." (verse 1 MSG) In the Greek language, *apostle* means, "one sent forth." Peter was a man of great faith who lived a radical life for Jesus Christ. He and the Apostle Paul were men on a mission to make disciples of Jesus. Peter writes this book "to exiles scattered to the four winds" (MSG).

The letter of First Peter was circulated to churches in the Asia Minor known as Pontus, Galatia, Cappadocia, Asia, and Bithynia. In this letter Peter states that we have a hope in Christ that's both for the present and the future.

Peter begins verse 3 by giving "praise" to the "God and Father of our Lord Jesus Christ!" Peter establishes that "in his great mercy he has given us new birth into a living hope." This "living hope" that derives from Christ's resurrection means that salvation is available for us today. Eternal life is not just waiting to die and go to heaven but recognizing that we can have an intimate and personal relationship with Jesus that begins here on earth. This new birth and living hope is not just a future hope—it's in the *present tense*, too.

Sometimes life is really *difficult*. Peter tells us that while we live in this world our faith will be tested to prove we are growing, and this testing will be used by God to lead us to a deep-seated faith. In this session, we will learn about the living hope we can have in Jesus.

Share
Warm-Up Questions

- What are some ways you greet friends? How do you greet strangers?

- What are some ways people exchange greetings in other cultures?

- How does it make you feel when someone sends you a hand-written letter?

Observe
Observation Questions

- Based on verses 1-3, what does Peter want the people to understand?

- Look at verses 4-5. What's Peter's message about God's power?

- In verses 6-9, what happens to those who withstand the testing of their faith?

- What do we learn about the Good News of salvation in verses 10-12?

Think
Interpretation Questions

- Why do you think God uses trust as the main way to connect with him?

- What do you think it means that hope is living?

- Why do you think some handle tests well and others fail?

- Why do you think that the prophets of old wanted to know more about salvation?

Apply

Application Questions

- How can doubt and hope and faith end up working together to make someone spiritually strong?

- What are some things that keep you from growing into this "living hope"?

- What are some ways to experience the "inexpressible joy" of following Jesus? (verse 8 NLT)

- How can you be a more faithful witness for Christ?

Do

Optional Activity

Have your group identify some of the things teens *hope* for. Write these down. Then decide if each hope is rooted in reality or fantasy. Then discuss what you think adults hope for. When you come up with a list, ask the questions: "Which of these are biblical hopes? Which are cultural?" Talk about the difference between hope and faith. Are *hoping* and *wishing* the same things? Is it okay to doubt? Why or why not? How can doubt benefit or hinder our faith? Discuss what it means to have "hope" based on God. Close in prayer.

QUIET TIME REFLECTIONS

Day 1: 1 Peter 1:1-3

- What word or phrase jumps out to you? Why?

- Why does the writer mention grace and peace? How do you define *grace*? *Peace*?

- Think about some ways to show grace and peace to others.

Day 2: 1 Peter 1:4-6

- How does this passage speak to you?

- What do you think Peter means when he says "an inheritance that can never perish, spoil or fade"?

- Think about why it's hard to rejoice when we "suffer grief in all kinds of trials."

Day 3: 1 Peter 1:7-8

- What insight do you gain from this text?

- Why do you think Peter is so excited about the end results of our faith being refined and tested? How did Peter experience this in his life?

- Think about how you've experienced this phrase: "Though you have not seen him (Jesus) you love him."

Day 4: 1 Peter 1:9-10

- What's one question you have about this passage?

- What does "you are receiving the end result of your faith, the salvation of your souls" mean?

- Think about why the prophets of old "who spoke of the grace that was to come to you, searched intently." What do we have today that those prophets did not have?

Day 5: 1 Peter 1:11

- What can you learn from this text?

- Why does Peter make a big deal about the prophets wanting to know of the fullness of the resurrected Christ?

- Peter tells us that the prophets of the Old Testament longed to know when and where the promised Savior would come. Why did they long for this? Do you long for Jesus to return today? Why or why not?

Day 6: 1 Peter 1:12

- What is God saying to you from this verse?

- Why do you think Peter says "even angels long to look into these things." What things is Peter speaking of?

- Think about some of the ways the Holy Spirit communicates with his people.

Day 7: 1 Peter 1:1-12

Read through the entire passage. Write down the **one verse** that spoke to you the most this week. Commit the verse to memory for an extra challenge!

12. WHAT IS HOLINESS?
1 Peter 1:13-2:1-10

LEADER'S INSIGHT

Some words are used sparingly these days—such as *holiness*.

As a young follower of Jesus, I heard older folks in the church joke about holiness using this saying: "We don't smoke or chew or run with those who do." It seemed to me in my late teens and early college days that holiness was more about what we *shouldn't do* rather than what we are called to do.

Holiness is being like Jesus. "But just as he who called you is holy, so be holy in all you do; for it is written: 'Be holy, because I am holy'." (verses 15-16) Holiness is a lifestyle, and teens need to know that we live in a sinful world with great pressures and temptations. Yet Christ calls us to live in the world system as lights (Philippians 2:15; John 17:14-15). We don't change the world by being like it; rather we change the world by being *different*.

What does holiness look like, practically? *First, we live our lives in reverence.* As we follow Jesus, we understand that holiness is living in awe and respect for God, seeking to please him with our obedience. *Secondly, we place our minds on Jesus.* 1 Peter 1:18-21 tells us that Jesus has delivered us from a futile way of life, and that we've been redeemed. In order to live a life of holiness, we put our thoughts on Christ and guard our minds from toxic influences. *Third, we crave the Word of God.* 1 Peter 2:1-3 says we grow in holiness by saturating ourselves in the Scriptures. Applying the Bible to our lives helps us grow and change and be molded into the image of Jesus. Why be holy? 1 Peter 2:9 tells us: We are chosen to live for God's glory. "You are a chosen people, a holy nation, a people belonging to God, that you may declare the praises of him who called you out of darkness into his wonderful light." Holiness is not primarily about what we don't do; it's about living to the high calling of being like Jesus.

Share

Warm-Up Questions

- What things come to mind when you hear the word holy or holiness?

- What do you consider the worst crime a person can commit?

- What's one of the best ways to make a difference in your community?

Observe

Observation Questions

- Based on 1 Peter 1:13-16, what are we being asked to do?

- In 1 Peter 1:17, what does it mean to fear God?

- What does the writer insist that we do in verse 22?

- What kinds of attitudes are we to put off and put on? (2:1-7)

Think

Interpretation Questions

- Why do you think God wants us to be holy?

- Why do you think God used blood as a sacrifice in the Old Testament and in the life of Jesus for the way of salvation?

- What do you think is the connection between God's love and his holiness?

- Why do you think that Jesus seems to cause such an uproar and reaction from people?

Apply

- What's one step you can take toward being holy like God?

- What are some ways to live in "reverent fear" of God?

- Who am I having trouble loving "deeply from the heart" and what can I do to change this?

- How will you grow spiritually in the Word? What plan will you choose to "crave pure spiritual milk"?

Do

Optional Activity

Consider an "Accountability Challenge in the Word." Check out this one-week plan:

- Have your group members read 1 Peter like a novel or book in one setting five times during the week.

- When you meet the next time, find out who succeeded. And then...

- Name one theme they picked up from their reading.

- Finally memorize one student's favorite verse.

QUIET TIME REFLECTIONS

Day 1: 1 Peter 1:13-16

- What word or phrase jumps out to you? Why?
- Why does the writer mention holiness in connection with self-control?
- Think about some ways you can demonstrate holiness to friends and family that make a difference.

Day 2: 1 Peter 1:17-21

- How does this passage speak to you?
- What do you think Peter means when he says that since God the Father "judges each man's work impartially, live your lives as strangers here in reverent fear"?
- Think about why it's hard sometimes to put our "faith and hope" in God?

Day 3: 1 Peter 1:22-25

- What insight do you gain from this text?
- Why do you think Peter stresses the lasting power of God's word and contrasts it with "all men are like grass" which withers and "flowers fall"?
- Think about some of the ways "the word of the Lord stands forever?"

Day 4: 1 Peter 2:1-3

- What's one question you have about the passage?
- What does it mean to "rid yourselves of all malice and all deceit, hypocrisy, envy, slander of every kind"? How can we pull this off?
- Think of some examples of how you've "tasted that the Lord is good."

Day 5: 1 Peter 2:4-6

- What can you learn from the text?

- Why does Peter speak about Jesus being chosen by God, yet rejected by people? What does this have to do with us?

- Think about how God has called you to be a living stone and follower of Jesus? What does that mean to you?

Day 6: 1 Peter 2:7-10

- What's God saying to you from these verses?

- Why do you think Peter talks about "to you who believe, this stone is precious"? Is this good news about Jesus still amazing to you or has it become ho-hum?

- Think about some of the ways God has rescued you from darkness and brought you into "his wonderful light."

Day 7: 1 Peter 1:13-2:1-10

Read through the entire passage. Write down the **one verse** that spoke to you the most this week. Commit the verse to memory for an extra challenge!

13. JESUS, OUR EXAMPLE
1 Peter 2:11-3:1-12

LEADER'S INSIGHT

Intergalactic battles?

Well, not exactly. But Peter does insist in this passage that we're to live as "aliens and strangers" in the current world system which stages an all-out war against our very souls. Living in this kind of world, under this intense pressure, calls for a radically different approach to life.

In this passage Peter begins with a general statement of what this type of alien lifestyle will look like for the believer. It's a life marked by abstinence and honor. This is the first secret to war against the "monster of the flesh." Don't feed the monster—deny it, deprive it, slay it with a life of honor and obedience to Christ. Our conduct ought to stand up to God's inspection and serve as a radical witness to those in the world around us.

Winning the war also requires a second radical weapon: Peter calls it "submission." This is an upside-down, far-sweeping weapon that flies directly in the face of the world system. Peter tells his readers to honor God, submit to the government, for servants to submit to their Masters—and for husbands and wives to submit to one another and to Christ. Just as Christ put the Father first in all he suffered, we are called to joyfully submit our lives under his authority and to those individuals or institutions he places us in as his personal representatives.

This is truly alien thinking and behavior according to the precepts of the enemy territory in which we reside. All day long we hear, *Fight for your rights! Me first! My way or the highway!* But as aliens and strangers in this world, Peter calls us to give up our rights and to live a new "alien" lifestyle with Christ.

Share
Warm-Up Questions

- What's your favorite "alien" movie or TV show?

- Have you ever thought about the fact that believers are called to live as "aliens" or strangers to this world? How comfortable are you with this thought? Explain.

- Are you more comfortable fitting in with those around you, or are you willing to stand out as a follower of Christ?

Observe
Observation Questions

- Read 1 Peter 2:11-12. What do these verses say it means to live an alien lifestyle?

- What does it mean to submit in 1 Peter 2:13-20?

- What does submission have to do with the way Jesus lived, according to 1 Peter 2:21-23?

- What two things does Peter connect in chapter 2:24-24 and chapter 3:1-7?

Think
Interpretation Questions

- Why do you think Peter uses the phrase "aliens and strangers" regarding how we're to live in this world?

- In 2:13-17 Peter talks about honoring the king and showing proper respect to everyone. How might you apply what he's saying to our modern, Western culture?

- Read 1 Peter 2:18-24. What impresses you about the way Jesus submitted to God's will and suffered for us?

- Read 1 Peter 3:8-12. How does Peter encourage us to respond to insults? Why would we want to act in a way that seems passive?

Apply

Application Questions

- What do you think it means to be submissive? Based on your definition, how can you achieve that?

- What are some practical ways to submit to authorities such as teachers, mentors, and parents?

- Who's someone you admire who's courageous in faith but also kind?

- If you were ever to marry, what one principle from 1 Peter 3:1-12 would you want to implement into your marriage?

Do

Optional Activity

Bring in some married couples for a panel discussion on marriage. Ask questions such as How did you meet? What is the best part of marriage? Toughest? What challenges have you faced? How do you implement faith into your marriage? What does it look like to "submit" to each other?

Following your time, have students ask questions about marriage and parenting. This can be a really helpful and defining discussion for students, even though they're perhaps years away from these kinds of decisions.

QUIET TIME REFLECTIONS

Day 1: 1 Peter 2:11-14

- What word or phrase jumps out to you? Why?

- What "sinful desires" do you face that "war against your soul"?

- Think about one simple way you can submit your life to God this week.

Day 2: 1 Peter 2:15-22

- How does this passage speak to you?

- What kind of suffering scares you? Does suffering ever lead to something positive? Can you think of an example?

- Think about how many people in certain countries and nations suffer physically. What's something you can do about it?

Day 3: 1 Peter 2:23-25

- What insight do you gain from this text?

- If someone hurls an insult at you, what do you usually do? Talk back? Walk away?

- Think about the way Jesus responded to torture. Why is it so hard not to retaliate?

Day 4: 1 Peter 3:1-5

- What's one question you have about this passage?

- What's the importance of inner beauty rather than external attraction?

- Think about how our culture focuses on looks, beauty, and having a perfect body. What should our response be?

Day 5: 1 Peter 3:6-8

- What can you learn from this text?

- What are some things you can do to demonstrate compassion and humility in your relationships with others?

- Think about someone in your school, or a neighbor who needs an act of compassion this week. Now go do it.

Day 6: 1 Peter 3:9-12

- What is God saying to you through these verses?

- When someone is mean to you, how can you refrain from responding with meanness?

- Think about giving a verbal blessing and encouragement this week to your parents at a time when they're not expecting it.

Day 7: 1 Peter 2:11-3:1-12

Read through the entire passage. Write down the **one verse** that spoke to you the most this week. Commit the verse to memory for an extra challenge!

14. GOOD SUFFERING
1 Peter 3:13-4:1-6

LEADER'S INSIGHT

No one looks forward to suffering.

You might say that suffering is the broccoli of faith: You don't want it, but you're getting it anyway because it's healthy.

The ongoing theme of 1 Peter is gaining endurance through suffering and persecution. The Christians, to whom Peter is writing, have endured affliction and distress. Some have lost their lives following Jesus. A common thought among many Christians today is that, because of their relationship with Christ, they should enjoy privileges in this life. Illness should occur rarely, if at all, and vanish quickly after faith-filled prayers. Calamity is for those "other" people who don't go to church. However, not only will Christians suffer—but suffering is actually part of God's will at times (3:17).

Of course that part of God's message has never been popular. John the Baptist was beheaded. The Apostle Paul endured numerous beatings, life-threatening situations, and shipwrecks. Even Jesus, the object of our faith, was arrested, beaten, and executed in a excruciating, humiliating way because he told people God's truth. The disturbing reality is that if the world opposed Jesus, we would deceive ourselves to believe we are headed for a kinder fate. The cross is still as offensive as it ever has been.

Hearing this, a Christian might be tempted to abandon hope. To profess love for Christ and submit ourselves to his will—and then suffer for it—seems unfair in every regard. Where is God in our hour of need? But the problem isn't with God; it's with our expectations.

It's like biting into a donut you thought was custard filled, only to discover it's filled with lemon (no, not the sweet filling...actual raw lemons). In the same way, suffering for the sake of Jesus leaves a bitter taste. So Peter wrote this letter to remind Christians that we'll be blessed in our suffering (3:14 NIV; Romans 5:1-5).

One would think that Peter would be apologetic for suffering (e.g., "Isn't it horrible we have to go through this?") But he isn't. Instead Peter tells us to welcome suffering head-on like Jesus, who suffered so that we might come to know God (3:18). In fact, rather than calling for God's judgment upon those who are antagonistic toward Christianity, Peter calls us to train (or "prepare," 3:15) ourselves to answer hard questions and enter debate with "gentleness and respect."

This is the very essence of the gospel, bringing a message of hope in Christ...even to those who may end up rejecting us.

Share

Warm-Up Questions

- Did you ever think you were buying one thing, but ended up with something else?

- Was there ever a time when you suffered for doing the right thing?

- Have you ever talked with someone about your Christian faith? What happened?

Observe

Observation Questions

- Read 1 Peter 3:13-17. What do we learn about suffering?

- What does 1 Peter 3:15 teach us about sharing our faith with others?

- Read 1 Peter 3:18. What does the suffering of Christ produce?

- Look at 1 Peter 4:1-6. How are we to live and what will be the result?

Think

Interpretation Questions

- Read 1 Peter 3:13-17. Why might suffering be good for us?

- Look at 1 Peter 3:15. Why do you think preparation and presentation are important in the defense of our faith?

- Read 1 Peter 3:18. Why do you think Peter draws our attention to the suffering of Christ?

- Look at 1 Peter 4:1-6. Why are Christians to live according to a different set of moral standards?

Apply

Application Questions

- How does it make you feel that suffering might be part of God's will for your life?

- While nobody enjoys suffering, what fruit might it bear in our lives?

- How have you prepared to defend your faith? Describe the last time you shared your faith. Were you able to share it with gentleness and respect?

- How can you draw strength from the model of Christ's suffering?

Do

Optional Activity

As a group, discuss ways you can prepare to defend your faith. Vote on your group's top three ideas. Choose one you'll apply this week. Each person should give permission to another person in the group to contact him or her in one week and ask what progress has been made (and vice versa). As a group pray for preparation, gentleness, and respect in declaring your faith to others.

QUIET TIME REFLECTIONS

Day 1: 1 Peter 3:13-14

- What word or phrase jumps out to you? Why?

- Have you ever had to suffer for what's right? How did God bless you in that experience or as a result of that experience?

- Christians are not supposed to be "frightened" (NIV translation) for standing up for what's right. Have you ever been afraid to stand up for what's right? What could you do the next time you're in that situation?

Day 2: 1 Peter 3:15-17

- How does this passage speak to you?

- Do you believe you are "prepared" (NIV translation) to share your faith? How can you be better prepared?

- Does your behavior stand in contrast to those who don't yet know Christ? Why or why not? Has it ever brought you suffering to stand up for what you believe?

Day 3: 1 Peter 3:18-22

- What insight do you gain from this text?

- In what way does suffering help us to identify with Jesus Christ? What was the purpose of his suffering?

- It's not baptism that saves us, but faith expressed through the act of baptism. Have you been baptized? Why or why not?

Day 4: 1 Peter 4:1-2

- What's one question you have about this passage?

- Think about the suffering of Christ. For whom did he suffer? Have you ever thought that Christians shouldn't suffer?

- Would you say your life is more focused on the will of God or your own desires? Where did Jesus get his strength for holy living? Where do we get our strength?

Day 5: 1 Peter 4:3-4

- What can you learn from this text?

- What activities are now in your past—or should be?

- Have you ever been pressured to compromise godly morals? What was the result? How will you handle this in the future?

Day 6: 1 Peter 4:5-6

- What is God saying to you through these verses?

- God will one day judge everyone. Do you ever wish that God's judgment would begin immediately? Why or why not? What is the benefit to God delaying that judgment?

- The point of the gospel is to offer rescue, through Christ, for those currently apart from God. How do you keep a Christ-like heart for those currently separated from God? What changes need to occur in your prayer life and daily activity to keep God's heart for those who need him?

Day 7: 1 Peter 3:13-4:6

Read through the entire passage. Write down the **one verse** that spoke to you the most this week. Commit the verse to memory for an extra challenge!

15. FIERY ORDEALS
1 Peter 4:7-19

LEADER'S INSIGHT

The early church leaders were radicals.

They wrote and lived with a sense of urgency, believing that the second coming of Christ would happen in their lifetimes. Peter was no different. He opens this section of Scripture saying, "The end of all things is near." We, just like Peter, should live in anticipation and expectancy of Christ's return. Peter provides practical methods for living in this manner. First of all he gives us guidelines for how we should pray, which are foundational to our faith. In order to pray, Peter tells us to be clear-minded and self-controlled (which is hard when so many of us struggle with attention-deficit disorder!).

There are times the devil wants to keep us distracted so that we're kept from building intimacy with God through prayer. Peter's remedy is to stay clear-minded and focused on God. In a culture inundated by 'round-the-clock news cycles, social media, and sound bites, it's difficult to stay focused amid the frenzy. Peter is telling us that if we desire a vibrant prayer life, we need to clear our minds of the things that distract us from intimate time with God. Next, Peter calls us to be self-controlled. How are you doing at managing day-to-day things? Are you losing the battle of your mind by allowing impure thoughts, bad habits, and poor choices to creep in? Peter is calling us to live a life that does not look unmanageable, but to be self-controlled. This is not a life built around using your own strength to live; Peter advocates using godly wisdom to make choices that allow you to live in a way that is holy or set apart.

Peter states we should "love each other deeply, because love covers over a multitude of sins." Not only does Peter provide the command to love, but also he lists ways we can live this out. Hospitality is a great way to express love and can take many forms—from hosting a small group and making people feel welcome in your home to visiting someone in the hospital and providing a meal to someone in need.

In verses 12 and following, Peter writes that God commands those who call themselves Christians to live obedient lives—and if we choose to follow this life, we will be objects of persecution from a world that does not share our values.

Many times the Christian life is presented as a picture of smiling faces sitting around a campfire roasting marshmallows and singing worship songs. We should not be surprised when we experience fiery trials, but rather should commit ourselves to following God and remain faithful to the one who has been faithful to us. God is able to use suffering for his good purpose and refine us into the godly men and women he desires us to be. Peter is clear that we shouldn't actively pursue suffering, but we should not run from it or be surprised when it happens to us.

Share

Warm-Up Questions

- If someone were to say to you that something was "near," what would that mean to you?

- What do you think of when you hear the word *suffering*?

- Should Christians be immune to suffering?

- What role, if any, should our faith play in suffering?

Observe

Observation Questions

- Read verse 7. What reason does the text give for being clear-minded and self-controlled?

- Read verses 10-11. What are the gifts to be used for?

- Read verses 12-13: What should our reaction be to suffering?

- Read verse 19: What should the believer continue to do?

Think

Interpretation Questions

- Read verses 7-11: How is God glorified through our use of the gifts he's given us?

- Read verse 12: Why should we not be surprised by painful trials or fiery ordeals we're suffering? Look at verses 15-16: How does suffering as a Christian differ from suffering as an unbeliever?

- Compare verse 18 with Proverbs 11:31. What is the significance of that verse? Why would Peter quote that verse here?

- Look at verse 19: Is it God's will that we should suffer? Why does Peter tell us to commit ourselves to God and continue to do well? Do you think this eases our suffering or brings more upon us?

Apply

Application Questions

- Why is being self-controlled and clearing your mind so important for prayer, and how do you do it?

- How can you ensure you're using your gifts to serve others, "faithfully administering God's grace?"

- What does it look like to rejoice in the face of suffering?

- How will you stay encouraged to continue to do good in the midst of suffering?

Do

Optional Activity

Write an encouraging note to a person undergoing a trial or suffering. Prepare a meal for him or her and deliver the note, along with the meal, in person. Commit to praying for that person whenever your group meets.

Visit the Voice of the Martyrs Web site: www.persecution.com. Pick a way for your church to get involved in helping our brothers and sisters being persecuted around the globe. Consider holding a fundraiser where the proceeds go to help this important ministry, or have your group write letters of encouragement to those imprisoned for the cause of Christ.

QUIET TIME REFLECTIONS

Day 1: 1 Peter 4:7-9

- What word or phrase jumps out to you? Why?

- What do you think Peter meant when he wrote, "The end of all things is near"?

- Why is it so important to be clear-minded and self-controlled? Ask God to show you one way you can love someone today and show hospitality to another person.

Day 2: 1 Peter 4:10-11

- How does this passage speak to you?

- What kind of "gift" is Peter writing about in verse 10?

- How can you make sure you're using your gifts in serving God? Consider talking to your youth leader about how to discover your spiritual gifts.

Day 3: 1 Peter 4:12-13

- What insight do you gain from this text?

- Do you think Peter tells us to expect suffering as though it's normal?

- What are some ways you can rejoice in the midst of suffering? Pray to God asking him to help you maintain a positive attitude of thankfulness whenever suffering happens. Ask for his help to endure through suffering.

Day 4: 1 Peter 4:14-16

- What's one question you have about this passage?

- Can you think of a time you were laughed at, picked on, or insulted because of your faith? How did you handle it?

- Is there anything you would do differently after studying this verse? Is there anything you are still holding on to, such as a grudge you need to forgive or something you need to be forgiven for?

Day 5: 1 Peter 4:17-18

- What can you learn from this text?

- What will be the outcome of the family of God? What about those who do not obey God?

- Read Proverbs 11:31. What's the significance of that verse? Why would Peter quote that verse here in verse 18?

Day 6: 1 Peter 4:19

- What is God saying to you through this verse?

- How have you seen God's faithfulness in your own life? Have you thanked him for this? What is God asking you to commit to?

- Will you consider sharing this with a friend or youth leader who can check in with you and ask you about your commitment you made to God?

Day 7: 1 Peter 4:7-19

Read through the entire passage. Write down the **one verse** that impacted you the most this week. Commit the verse to memory for an extra challenge!

16. THE FLOCK OF GOD
1 Peter 5:1-14

LEADER'S INSIGHT

Know why buffet-style restaurants are popular?

Because people love having 30 to 50 options to satisfy their appetites. Most buffets have a range of ice cream, fruit, gourmet breads, steak, chicken, seafood, rices, vegetables, sides, and desserts. There is something for everyone. No one walks out of a buffet saying, "Boy I'm full, but I wish they had offered pinto beans." Most people say, "Why did I eat so much?" They're not thinking about the specifics of what they ate—simply the quantity.

Now imagine if a restaurant offered a buffet, but instead of the normal chef preparing the food, they called in a world-renowned chef. Can you picture the headlines? "Famous chef hired by Joe's Buffet to refine their fried chicken." As humorous as it is to think of the most qualified chef with loads of credentials and experience taking on this job, no one would be laughing once they tasted the chicken. The entire buffet would be enhanced by the skill and expertise of the chef.

Much like a buffet, Peter offers a wide variety of teachings in this passage, and there is something for everyone. No matter what you're going through or what you're "craving," something will hit the spot. In this case Peter is the master chef we imagined earlier. Right at the beginning of the passage (verse 1) he establishes his credentials: a fellow elder, witness of the sufferings of Christ, and partaker in the glory. Peter is not just a believer in Jesus—he's one of the most experienced Christians of that time. He's beyond qualified and therefore should be listened to. But Peter isn't only teaching Christian etiquette in these verses; it's etiquette for pastors—for the shepherds.

So if you're a leader in any capacity, with influence and the desire to impact others, listen to these verses. This is your instruction manual—your five-star buffet.

Share

Warm-Up Questions

- Do you enjoy school? Why or why not?

- Do you have a really good teacher? What makes him/her good?

- Have you ever been a teacher? If so, what was that like?

- What's something you're good at and could teach others?

Observe

Observation Questions

- Read verses 1-5. Who does Peter address first? What does Peter make a point of mentioning here?

- Read verses 2-9. How many commands does Peter give his readers?

- Read verses 10-11. What's the purpose of these sufferings? Who is to be honored?

- Read verses 12-14. What do you notice about the closing of this letter in regard to the body of Christ? (Hint: Does it sound like a family?)

Think

Interpretation Questions

- Based on verses 1-5, what are the expectations for pastors and young members of a church? How should they act?

- Look at verses 6-11. Why do you think Peter includes Satan in the midst of our behaviors and attitudes? How does Peter describe him?

- Look at verses 12-14. Why do you think Peter ends with wishing peace to all who are in Christ?

- What does peace have to do with Jesus?

Apply

Application Questions

- Evaluate your own leadership. Hold up verses 1-5 as a test to see how well you're matching up to a biblical leader and learner.

- How do we realistically resist the Devil? Does this passage offer any clues?

- Compared to the list of things that Peter gives, what in your life needs to be changed or tweaked?

- Are you seeking peace in your life through Jesus Christ? If you were to receive peace, what would that look like?

Do

Optional Activity

Have your group identify all the qualities Peter expects of leaders and followers in this passage. Give each member of your group 20 *fake* dollars and hold an auction for each attribute (e.g., oversight, willingness, eagerness, humbleness, etc.) in which the students will bid on what they think is most important. Once the auction is complete, take time to debrief and allow each student to share why he or she put emphasis on that particular attribute. What about it stood out? Why do you think that's important? Use this time to help them see why they value certain things, but also to understand Peter's emphasis and expectation on these qualities in relation to a leader or follower.

QUIET TIME REFLECTIONS

Day 1: 1 Peter 5:1-4

- What word or phrase jumps out at you? Why?

- How do Peter's credentials in verse 1 affect the words he writes? Do they help you buy into what he's saying?

- Look at the phrase "not domineering over those in your charge" in verse 3. (ESV) When you're put in leadership roles, or even when you're hanging out with your friends, do you use your power in helpful ways or hurtful ways?

Day 2: 1 Peter 5:5

- How does this passage speak to you?

- Would you say sometimes you have a hard time listening to and obeying those older than you? Why?

- What do you think it means to have humility toward one another? Do you struggle with this in your life? What can you do to change this?

Day 3: 1 Peter 5:6-7

- What insight do you gain from this text?

- What do you think it means that God will exalt you at the proper time? Can you think of another biblical example of humility leading to exalting?

- Do you struggle with worry? Do you really think it's possible to cast all your anxieties upon God? Do you really believe God cares for you? Why/why not?

Day 4: 1 Peter 5:8-9

- What's one question you have about this passage?

- What do you think it means to be sober-minded and watchful? Why is that important in regard to the Devil?

- Do you think it's hard to stand firm in your faith? Why or why not?

- How does it help your walk with Christ to know that other Christians around the world are going through the same temptations as you?

Day 5: 1 Peter 5:10-11

- What can you learn from this text?

- Have you ever suffered for your faith? What are some ways Christians in other parts of the world suffer for their faith?

- Is there hope in the midst of suffering? What does Peter say will be the final result of suffering?

Day 6: 1 Peter 12-14

- What's God saying to you from these verses?

- Peter encourages us again to stand firm in the grace of God (ESV) at the end of his letter. What do you think that means? How is this accomplished?

- The last part of Peter's letter is about peace. What areas of your life aren't "at peace" right now? To what things do you need to apply the peace of Christ?

Day 7: 1 Peter 5:1-14

Read through the entire passage. Write down **one verse** that spoke to you the most this week. Commit the verse to memory for an extra challenge!

17. WHAT IS A CALLING?
2 Peter 1:1-11

LEADER'S INSIGHT

Do you like to eat home-baked cookies straight from the oven?

Most of us do (as long as they aren't burnt, of course). A lot of work goes into a perfectly baked dessert, but it all begins with a recipe. Inside every cookie or cake is a list of ingredients that are added at just the right time and in the right measure. When each part is combined with the others and placed in the oven, the outcome is a perfectly planned treat.

Peter is writing to a group of believers, who, like himself, are wondering who God wants them to be and whether they have the "ingredients" to fulfill the desired outcome. Peter's attention is given to our "call" as Christians—our purpose in life. In verse 3, Peter answers the question by saying "we have been given everything we need for life and Godliness." God will provide all we need to fulfill our ultimate purpose, a life of godliness.

So what are the "ingredients" that go into the making of a good life? The writer says we start with a base of faith. We begin with trusting in God's grace. We add to that goodness and knowledge. Our height of salvation should correlate with a depth of knowledge of Jesus through studying his Word. A dash of self-control ensures that we're diligent in obeying God's instructions in our life. Without self-control we can never have the next ingredient, which is perseverance. Self-control allows us to finish well. Godliness, brotherly kindness, and love are the last three items mixed in. When we become godly in our dealings with others, we begin to display brotherly kindness and real

Christian love. The kicker is that these items aren't added once; in verse 8 Peter states these ingredients must be added again and again.

Peter assures his readers that God has a purpose and a call for each of us. God's desire is for each of us to become obedient to him and receive a rich welcome into his kingdom. God is so serious about this call that he promises to provide all that we need to achieve it. Our heavenly father is a great chef and we're his creation. In this session we'll learn how to become the people God wants us to be.

Share

Warm-Up Questions

- What's your favorite thing to cook or bake? Why?

- What happens if you don't get all the ingredients correct while cooking or baking? Has that ever happened to you?

- Have you ever wondered why God has placed you on this earth?

Observe

Observation Questions

- Read 1:1. What has allowed Peter's readers to receive the "faith" so precious to them?

- Examine 1:3-4. What provides us the things we need to live godly lives? What does it allow us to escape?

- According to 1:8, what happens if we possess in "increasing measure" the qualities listed in verses 5-7?

- In 1:9, what would cause us to neglect growing in these qualities?

Think

Interpretation Questions

- Why is knowledge of Jesus Christ so important, and why is it mentioned four times in 11 verses?

- What things does God provide through his power for our calling to be godly?

- How would you define each of the "ingredients" listed in verses 5-7 (i.e., faith, goodness, knowledge, self-control, perseverance, godliness, brotherly kindness, love)?

- What's the danger of forgetting we've been cleansed from sin? Why might it keep us from growing in the character qualities Peter lists?

Apply

Application Questions

- What in your life would suggest that your faith is as precious to you as it was to the readers of this letter?

- Are there times you make excuses for not fulfilling your calling and purpose and not living a godly life? What are the excuses?

- Name one way you can practically add the ingredients from verses 5-7 to your life today? (i.e., faith, goodness, knowledge, self-control, perseverance, godliness, brotherly kindness, love)

- Does knowing God's ultimate call and purpose for you to be godly change your view of your purpose on earth? If so, how?

Do

Optional Activity

As a group write a "recipe" for God's call on your lives. Read through the ingredients from verses 5-7 and write out potential action steps to increase these in your lives. For instance, what's a practical way to increase your knowledge of Jesus Christ? Make an effort to write down amount and frequency for the desired outcome. Trust that God will provide all you need to live a godly life.

QUIET TIME REFLECTIONS

Day 1: 2 Peter 1:1-2

- What word or phrase jumps out to you? Why?

- Why does Peter mention Jesus three times in these two verses?

- Does the knowledge of Jesus Christ bring you grace and peace? Why or why not?

Day 2: 2 Peter 1:3

- How does this passage speak to you?

- What does it mean that God has "called" us by his own glory and goodness?

- Where do you need God's power in your life to continue pursuing godliness?

Day 3: 2 Peter 1:4

- What insight do you gain from this text?

- What precious promises has God given us through his word?

- How do evil desires cause corruption in the world? Why is God so intent on us being rescued from that?

Day 4: 2 Peter 1:5-7

- What's one question you have about this passage?

- Do you see a progression or process to these ingredients listed? If so, what's the process?

- What's significant about the last ingredient being love?

Day 5: 2 Peter 1:8-9

- What can you learn from this text?

- How do these ingredients keep us from being ineffective in our knowledge of Jesus Christ?

- What past sins have you been forgiven from? Thank God for all he's done for you.

Day 6: 2 Peter 1:10-11

- What's God saying to you through these verses?

- As a Christian and follower of Jesus, you have now been called and elected—how can you be eager to live this out?

- What does Peter promise us as a reward if we live with confident knowledge that we belong to Jesus and are called by him?

Day 7: 2 Peter 1:1-11

Read through the entire passage. Write down the **one verse** that spoke to you the most this week. Commit the verse to memory for an extra challenge!

18. POWER OF THE BIBLE
2 Peter 1:12-21

LEADER'S INSIGHT

"You can't handle the truth!" is a classic line from the movie, *A Few Good Men.*

But Peter knew that if we can't handle the truth, life will handle us. Peter was dedicated and passionate about making sure God's people understand the truth. Why? Peter wants us to remember the truth so when we're under attack by false teachers, we know where to gain stability, security, and authority.

In verses 16-21, we see Peter's heart for writing this letter. First he mentions the transfiguration of Jesus Christ in verses 16-18 and then the power of Scripture to undergird our lives. The Bible isn't a collection of stories invented by human ideas, but as Peter says, "We were eyewitnesses of his majesty" (verse 16) and "no prophecy of Scripture came about by the prophets' own interpretation." (verse 20)

Verse 19: "Because of that, we have *greater confidence* (my emphasis) in the message proclaimed by the prophets. Pay close attention to what they wrote, for their words are like a light shining in a dark place—until the day of Christ appears and his brilliant light shines in your hearts."(NLT) The brilliant light shining in your hearts is the power of God helping us understand God's Word. The Bible is that light for us until Christ returns. The Holy Spirit illuminates the written word of God so that it gives us direction and guidance on how to really live.

It's important to grasp just how powerful the Bible really is—that the Holy Spirit illuminates it. As we see in verses 20-21, the Bible was not written by the will of man but "men spoke from God as they were carried along by the Holy Spirit."

In 2 Timothy 3:16-17, the apostle Paul writes that the Scriptures are "inspired" from God, or literally "God breathed." At the time of its writing, what we know as the New Testament did not yet exist; so when New Testament authors use the word "Scripture" we need to understand they are referring to the entire Old Testament writings from Genesis to Malachi. The men and women who penned the words of Scripture were inspired by God to write down his sayings. Peter tells us that even though he audibly heard the voice of God from heaven on the Mount of Transfiguration (Matthew 17:1-10), today we have an even more authoritative word in the Holy Scriptures for life and faith.

Share

Warm-Up Questions

- What are you most passionate about? Why?

- What are you least passionate about?

- Are you passionate about reading your Bible? How would you define passion? What are some ways to become passionate?

Observe

Observation Questions

- Based on verses 13-15, what does Peter mean when he instructs us to "put aside" or to "depart"?

- Look at verse 16. What might Peter have had in mind when he talked about being an eyewitness to Christ's majesty?

- In verse 17b, what phrase does Peter use to describe God? What do these two words mean and why does he put them together?

- Look at verse 21. What is important about the Holy Spirit here?

Think

- What are "these things" (verse 12) that Peter wants us to remember? Why do you think it's so important for us to remember them?

- What do you think Peter is referring to when he says the "day dawns" and "the morning star rises in your hearts" at the end of verse 19?

- What do you learn about the Bible in verses 19-21? Explain.

- Why do you think Peter wanted us to know that the Bible wasn't written by man's will but by the Holy Spirit?

Apply

Application Questions

- What have you found helpful for actually applying what you learn in the Bible to your personal life and your own struggles?

- What are some distractions or commitments in your life right now that are keeping you from reading the Bible?

- What can you do to limit those hindrances so you're able to experience more of the power of the Bible?

Do

Optional Activity

Bible Ladder involves putting things in order. Each team gets a stack of index cards with various biblical events written on them, and students must put them in order of when they happen in the Bible. Create index cards and place tape or Velcro on the backs of the cards so students can place them on a board. As a student places an event on the board, talk about how that event is significant in the overarching storyline of the Bible, leading to Jesus.

QUIET TIME REFLECTIONS

Day 1: 2 Peter 1:12-13

- What word or phrase jumps out to you? Why?
- How well do you know the basic truths of the Bible?
- Are you reading the Bible on a regular basis? If not, then why not?

Day 2: 2 Peter 1:14-15

- How does this passage speak to you?
- What would you do if you knew your death was coming soon?
- Where do you think you will go after death?

Day 3: 2 Peter 16

- What insight do you gain from this text?
- Why do people invent stories to explain what they do not understand? How does the Bible differ from stories that people invent?
- Imagine what it would've been like to witness Jesus' earthly life. If you could choose one event from the life of Jesus to witness, which would it be? Why?

Day 4: 2 Peter 17-18

- What's one question you have about this passage?
- Would you be frightened or joyful if you heard God's voice? Why?
- What does it mean to say that Jesus is the Son of God? How would you explain this to someone else?

Day 5: 2 Peter 19

- What can you learn from this text?

- Are you paying attention to the words of the prophets during dark times in your life?

- How excited are you for the day of the rising of the Morning Star when Jesus comes again? Why or why not?

Day 6: 2 Peter 20-21

- What's God saying to you through these verses?

- What does Peter say about the prophet's interpretation of Scripture?

- Who was side by side with the prophets as they wrote? Why is this important?

Day 7: 2 Peter 12-21

Read through the entire passage. Write down the **one verse** that spoke to you the most this week. Commit the verse to memory for an extra challenge!

19. TOP 10 WAYS TO KNOW IF YOU ARE A FALSE TEACHER
2 Peter 2:1-22

LEADER'S INSIGHT

How do you know if something is true or false?

Have you ever wondered whether certain communicators at your church, youth conference, or retreat were "false teachers"? Worse yet, what if *you* fell into that category? Peter speaks to this issue by defining who and what qualifies as a "false teacher." Considering all the end-times prophets, prosperity gospel pushers, hell-erasers, and turn-or-burn preachers these days, it would be good to know God's criteria for a false teacher.

Peter knew the importance of recognizing false teachers because of the destruction they caused in the church. Peter, while awaiting his martyrdom in Rome, wrote a short, three-chapter letter to the church, and one chapter dealt with "false teachers." The ancient near east was no stranger to wrong thinking about God, and because of that Peter has much to teach us today about false teachers.

If Peter had a late-night TV show, he might have his own top-10 list:

You Know You're a False Teacher If You...

10. Secretly bring in destructive lies. (verse 1)

9. Lead a life of sensualities. (verse 2)

8. Use people of the church for personal gain. (verse 2)

7. Live a life of lustful passion. (verse 10)

6. Hate authority. (verse 10)

5. Have no fear of the spiritual realm. (verse 10)

4. Revel in deception. (verse 13)

3. Have eyes full of adultery. (verse 14)

2. Entice unsteady souls. (verse 14)

1. Cause confusion. (verse 17)

Because we live in a time of snap judgments, we must be careful when using the label *false teacher*. The term carries more than just bad theology. According to Peter it also means willful deception and immorality.

The word *theology* means "the study of God." Everyone has a theology of God whether they know it or not. When people move away from the Scriptures, they open themselves into the potential of accepting weird ideas. Orthodox Christians refer to this as *heresy*—or as the *Free Dictionary* defines it: "an opinion or doctrine contrary to the orthodox tenets of a religious body or church."

Chances are you'll meet lots of people who don't think like you. But deal with people who have an incorrect understanding of Scripture in the same way Christ deals with them—with patience and grace. Not with a pitchfork and torch!

Share

Warm-Up Questions

- Name a time when someone misunderstood you. How did it feel?

- What philosophy or teaching have you heard from someone older than you that didn't make any sense?

- Describe a situation in which you had to challenge something you thought was incorrect.

Observe

- Read 2:1-3. How does this text describe "false teachers"?

- Look at 2:4-10a. What four examples does Peter use for rescuing the godly and judging the unrighteous?

- Read verses 10b-18. In what other ways does Peter describe "false teachers"?

- Read verses 19-22. Why does Peter say it will be worse for the "false teachers"?

Think

Interpretation Questions

- Based on verse 9 (and see James 1:2), why didn't God just eliminate all the false teachers?

- Look at verse 17. Why do you think Peter described "false teachers" as waterless springs and mists?

- In verse 21, why do you think it's better for one to never have known the way of righteousness?

Apply

Application Questions

- What criteria would you use to judge whether someone is a false teacher?

- How would you respond to a fellow Christian who disagrees with your view on any spiritual matter?

- Are there some traits you sometimes share with false teachers? Does that make you a false teacher? Why/why not?

- After studying this passage, how has your perspective changed on the topic of false teachers?

Do

Optional Activity

In your group reflect on a time when you've been misunderstood and how that felt. Then consider a time when you've made a snap judgment that was totally wrong. As a group, talk about the danger of making snap judgments and ways we can do a better job of understanding what others are saying.

QUIET TIME REFLECTIONS

Day 1: 2 Peter 2:1-3

- What word or phrase jumps out to you? Why?

- Have you ever met or heard of someone you thought was a false teacher?

- Think of a way you've been exploited by someone or taken advantage of. What lies did they use to get you to do what they wanted?

Day 2: 2 Peter 2:4-6

- How does this passage speak to you?

- Spend some time thinking about God's judgment for the unrighteous.

- Read more about the angels that rebelled against God in Jude 6. Jude speaks of them abandoning their positions of authority. Where does all authority come from, ultimately?

Day 3: 2 Peter 2:7-9

- What insight do you gain from this text?

- Spend some time thinking about how God rescues the righteous.

- How is our salvation from sin similar to Lot's rescue from Sodom and Gomorrah?

Day 4: 2 Peter 2:10-14

- What's one question you have from this passage?

- What do you think Peter means by "blaspheming the glorious ones"? (ESV) And why is it a big deal?

- What sins describing false teachers do you find particularly awful? Why?

Day 5: 2 Peter 2:15-18

- What can you learn from this passage?

- What do you think Peter means by "forsaking the right way"? (ESV)

- What do you learn about Balaam in Numbers 22:21-41?

Day 6: 2 Peter 2:19-22

- What is God saying to you through these verses?

- What people do false teachers like to entice?

- Spend some time considering the phrase "for whatever overcomes a person, to that he is enslaved." (ESV) How is that true in your life?

Day 7: 2 Peter 2:1-22

Read through the entire passage. Write down the **one verse** that spoke to you the most this week. Commit the verse to memory for an extra challenge!

20. THE DAY OF THE LORD
2 Peter 3:1-18

LEADER'S INSIGHT

People love to think about the end times. The last chapter in Peter's "letter" (known as an *epistle* and written by an *apostle*) is dedicated almost entirely to "last days" (verse 3) and "the day of the Lord." (verse 10) Peter knows there are many weird ideas floating around regarding the "day of the Lord," that day when Christ will return and judge the world, so he writes to clear up any misconceptions.

The layout of the letter is fairly simple:

Words of the Present (2 Peter 3:3-4). Peter mentions "scoffers" who will mock the idea of the coming of Christ. They will ask, "Where is this coming he promised?" These skeptics question the validity of Jesus' return.

Words from the past (3:5-6). Peter takes his readers to the creation of the world and the Flood as evidence of God's power.

Back to the Future (3:7). It's logical to conclude his argument by citing "by the same word" that created the world and also used a flood to destroy it (Genesis 6); the future will be renovated by fire.

Peter concludes his letter by explaining the mysteries of the end times, the day of the Lord, and the final judgment. Let's discover what we can learn about the day of the Lord.

Share
Warm-Up Questions

- Have you heard any crazy ideas about the end of the world? If so, what are they?

- Does the end of the world worry or concern you in any way?

- What do you think happens to you when you die?

Observe
Obervation Questions

- Based on 2 Peter 3:1-3, what are some skeptics saying about the end times?

- What does Peter say in verses 4-7 about the end of the world?

- What do you learn about God in verses 8-13?

- According to verses 14-18, what are we to do in light of the coming of Christ?

Think
Interpretation Questions

- Why do you think people scoff and are skeptical of the last days?

- What is Peter meaning by "with the Lord a day is like a thousand years, and a thousand years are like a day"?

- What do you learn about God's patience and his desire for "everyone to come to repentance"?

- What does it mean to repent?

Apply
Application Questions

- How can you resist being skeptical about the end times?

- What's one way you can practice living a holy and godly life?

- Who can you be praying for to encounter Jesus?

- Peter mentions to be on guard from error and falling from "your secure position." What's one thing you can do to guard yourself against this?

Do

Optional Activity

Have your students interview friends and family members about the end times. Here are some possible questions:

- Do you believe the world will end? If yes, what will it look like? If no, what happens to the earth?

- Do you believe in a rapture or second coming of Christ? Why or why not?

- If you do believe in the return of Jesus, do you think Christ will return in our lifetime?

Bring your answers back to the group the following week and share them.

QUIET TIME REFLECTIONS

Day 1: 2 Peter 3:1-3

- What word or phrase jumps out to you? Why?

- Why does the writer mention scoffers in terms of the end times?

- Think about some ways to discuss the end times with friends.

Day 2: 2 Peter 3:4-7

- How does this passage speak to you?

- What do you think Peter means when he says "ungodly men" will be judged and destroyed? Does this mean eternal punishment (i.e., fire and brimstone) or annihilation (i.e., soul sleep)?

- Think about why there is a judgment for all people? Does this seem fair? How many judgments will there be?

Day 3: 2 Peter 3:8-10

- What insight do you gain from this text?

- What do you think Peter means by, "He (God) is patient with you, not wanting anyone to perish, but everyone to come to repentance"?

- Think about some of your friends and family members who have not yet responded to Jesus' love. Take time to pray for them today.

Day 4: 2 Peter 3:11-13

- What's one question you have about this passage?

- What does Peter mean by, "You ought to live holy and godly lives as you look forward to the day of God and speed its coming"? How can we speed up the coming of Christ?

- Think about Peter's question in verse 11: "What kind of people ought you to be?" What kind of person should you be?

Day 5: 2 Peter 3:14-15

- What can you learn from this text?

- Why does Peter say "make every effort to be found spotless, blameless, and at peace with him (God)"? How can God help with this?

- Think about how God's "patience means salvation" and what that means in your life.

Day 6: 2 Peter 3:16-18

- What is God saying to you through these verses?

- Why do you think Peter closes his letter with a warning of falling?

- Think about ways to grow in the grace and knowledge of Jesus that excite you.

Day 7: 2 Peter 3:1-18

Read through the entire passage. Write down the **one verse** that spoke to you the most this week. Commit the verse to memory for an extra challenge!

Part 3

The Letters of First, Second, and Third John

HANDY INSIGHTS AND TIPS ON FIRST, SECOND, AND THIRD JOHN

WHO? The writer of First, Second, and Third John is John the beloved (one of Jesus' original 12 followers). John wrote these books in the New Testament:

- The **Gospel of John**, the fourth book in the New Testament following Matthew, Mark, and Luke.

- **First, Second, and Third John** (toward the end of the New Testament)

- **The Book of Revelation**, the final book of the Bible.

WHERE? Most scholars believe these three letters were written toward the end of the apostle's life from the city of Ephesus. John was perhaps the only disciple of Jesus who died of natural causes. Many of the disciples were killed or martyred for their faith. John died of old age, probably on the Isle of Patmos (where he penned the book of Revelation).

WHEN? John wrote many of his letters later in life, probably between A.D. 80-90.

WHAT? John was writing to *Jesus people* everywhere to understand the simple truth of Christian faith: love God and people. Starting back in Deuteronomy 6:4 the text says "love the Lord your God with all your heart and with all your soul and with all your strength." The Jewish community refers to the passage as the *shema*. Years later when Jesus came on the scene, he was asked by an expert in the *Torah* (the first five books of Moses), "Of all the commandments, which is the most important?" (Mark 12:28) It was a profound question, because the scholar wanted to know out of the *613* commandments in the Old Testament, which was the most vital. Jesus affirmed Deuteronomy 6 as the final answer. But then he added one more text, an obscure verse in Leviticus 19:18b: "You shall love your neighbor as yourself." John's letters (1, 2, and 3) are a reaffirmation of Deuteronomy 6:4 and Leviticus 19:18. The most important value in life is to love God (vertical) and love people (horizontal).

1 John can be broken down into these themes:

- Chapter 1: Light
- Chapter 2: Truth
- Chapter 3: Love
- Chapter 4: Life
- Chapter 5: Believe

2 John: Love and Truth

3 John: Words of Advice

21. THE WORD LIVED IN THE NEIGHBORHOOD
1 John 1:1-10

LEADER'S INSIGHT

The Christian faith isn't always easy to understand.

One of the most incredible mysteries is mentioned in John's Gospel, chapter 1, verse 1: "In the beginning was the Word, and the Word was with God, and the Word was God." When we jump down to John 1:14, it reads, "The Word became flesh and made his dwelling among us." *God became human.* I cannot seem to wrap my mind around this incredible truth.

John continues this thought in his letters of 1, 2, and 3 John. In 1 John 1:1, we read "That which was from the beginning, which we have heard, which we have seen with our eyes, which we have looked at and our hands have touched—this we proclaim concerning the Word of Life."

Notice the words "we have seen with our eyes" and "our hands have touched" are symbols from John, saying "This God who became man, we got to hang out with him and spend time with him and watch him do miracles and see him sleep and fish and cast out evil spirits and heal people and interact with sick people and debate with the rabbis and religious leaders. We were with this Jesus. He was a real living person." John is taking something that is "out there" and making it practical and real. "The life appeared; we have seen it." (verse 2) John saw Jesus; he lived with Jesus for three years. Then, following Jesus' death and resurrection, he appeared "to all the apostles." (1 Corinthians 15:8)

God came to the planet as a human being. "He came and lived in the neighborhood." (John 1:14 MSG) In this first chapter of 1 John, we will dive more into the mystery of the incarnation, God becoming man and how that will help our students deal with light, darkness, sin, and forgiveness.

John is saying that Jesus is *experiential*. One of the reasons some are bored with church and Christianity is that they are dying to experience Christ, but their experience isn't happening. That can lead to frustration and disappointment. The good news is that God came to earth in the person of Jesus to live in our neighborhood and transform our lives from ordinary to extraordinary. This is what session 21 is all about.

Share

Warm-Up Questions

- Where has been one of the greatest places you've ever visited? What made that experience so exciting and/or fun?
- What is one life experience you've never had (e.g., skydiving, travel, scuba diving, etc.) that you'd like to have in the next five years?

Observe

Observation Questions

- Based on verses 1-4, what does John say about his experience with Jesus?
- Read verses 5-7. What contrast does John make as he talks about walking? What is the difference between these two ways of walking?
- In verse 8, what does it mean to be deceptive?
- What do we learn about forgiveness and cleansing in verses 9-10?

Think
Interpretation

- Why do you think John calls Jesus "the Word of Life"?

- What two reasons does John give for proclaiming Jesus as the word of life? (verse 3)

- What do you think it means to "walk in the light as he is in the light"? (verse 7)

- Why is it important to confess our sins if God already knows them? (verse 9)

Apply
Application

- John talks about those who claim to walk with God but are actually walking in darkness. Can a person know God and yet consistently choose to sin? What do you think John would say?

- What assurance does John give us for believing that Jesus truly forgives our sins? (verse 7) How can knowing this help you say no to sin in your life?

- What are some ways to have fellowship with God and people? (verses 7-9) Is this a priority in your life?

- How can you really know you are forgiven of your sins? (verse 9)

Do
Optional Activity

Contact a nursing home or elderly care/assisted-living facility to see if your group can serve for a few hours. Jesus came to serve, and his mission was primarily to the "least of these." Have your students serve and then afterward discuss it.

- "What was the experience like for you?"

- "How did you feel about the time here?"

- "Would you like to do this again? Why or why not?"

Students learn best when they have an experience and then debrief it. Connect the dots about how and why *experience* is so important, especially when it relates to being a follower of Jesus. Dialogue about what it means to be a light to the world. Talk about how Jesus came and lived in the neighborhood. Pray together to catch a vision to meet people with real needs with lasting impact.

QUIET TIME REFLECTIONS

Day 1: 1 John 1:1

- What word or phrase jumps out to you? Why?

- Why does the writer mention his past experience with Jesus? Why is that important for us who have never seen Jesus?

- Think about some ways you have experienced the risen Jesus.

Day 2: 1 John 1:2

- How does this passage speak to you?

- What do you think is the relevance of John saying, "We have seen it and testify to it"?

- Think about what it takes to believe and trust in Jesus when you have never seen him.

Day 3: 1 John 1:3-4

- What insight do you gain from this text?

- What does it mean to have "fellowship with us, and our fellowship is with the Father and with his Son, Jesus Christ"? (verse 3)

- Think about some of the amazing joys that come from encountering this God-man Jesus.

Day 4: 1 John 1:5-6

- What is one question you have about this passage?

- What does it mean that "God is light; in him there is no darkness"?

- Think about what this verse means: "We are lying if we say we have fellowship with God but go on living in spiritual darkness." (NLT) What does it mean to walk in darkness?

Day 5: 1 John 1:7-8

- What can you learn from this text?

- What is the outcome of "walking in the light" based on verses 7-8?

- Think about some of the mistakes and poor choices you've made and sins you've committed. Take a few moments to remember the good news that Jesus died so that you can be forgiven. (verse 7)

Day 6: 1 John 1:9-10

- What is God saying to you from these verses?

- What is the result of confessing our sins to God based on 1 John 1:9?

- Think about some of the times you confessed sins to God and still felt guilty. What will it take to believe God that he forgives and cleanses all your sins?

Day 7: 1 John 1:1-10

Read through the entire passage. Write down the **one verse** that spoke to you the most this week. Commit the verse to memory for an extra challenge!

22. CALLED TO LOVE
1 John 2:1-11

LEADER'S INSIGHT

Eugene Peterson says the two most difficult things to get straight in life are "love and God."

"More often than not, the mess people make of their lives can be traced to failure or stupidity or meanness in one or both of these areas." (*The Message*: The New Testament in Contemporary English, page 345, 1993.)

God speaks through the apostle John as we read these three letters (1, 2, 3 John) urging God's people to get this calling right, to love deeply. In chapter 2, John provides hope to guide God's people out of sinful decisions and into a right relationship with God. Jesus came to resolve the sin barrier between God and his creatures. Jesus is the "atoning sacrifice for our sins." (2:2)

Love and obedience are interconnected. Ask parents who are trying to teach their kids the importance of love and obedience. Our love for God is revealed not through words, but actions. "We know that we have come to know him if we keep his commands." (2:4) Jesus says in John 15:14, "You are my friends if you do what I command." Love is a verb, and obedience is the outcome of our friendship with God.

"Whoever says, 'I know him,' but does not do what he commands is a liar, and the truth is not in that person. But if anyone obeys his word, love for God is truly made complete in them. This is how we know we are in him: Whoever claims to live in him must live as Jesus did." (2:4-6)

"Live as Jesus did" is the crux for students to embrace. It's not about the meetings we attend, or how many camps, retreats, and mission trips we've been on; it's about living as Jesus did. To love is to live in the light; to hate a brother or sister (verse 9) is to live in darkness. There is no stumbling in the light (verse 10). Hate is living in darkness. Hate blinds us. We are called to love like Jesus, who loved the disenfranchised, the despised of his culture. Are you walking in light or the darkness?

Share

Warm-Up Questions

- What are some ways we can know that someone loves us? How can we show love to others?

- What communicates love most clearly to you? Perhaps it's words or acts of service or sharing time together? Talk about some of the different ways love can be expressed.

- What person, other than Jesus, do you think of when you look for an example of what love truly means?

Observe

Observation Questions

- Reading verses 1-4, what connection does John make between love and obedience?

- Read verses 5-8. How does John say we know that we are truly living in obedience to Jesus? What should our life and love look like?

- In verse 9, what does it mean to hate someone?

- In verses 9-11, how does John connect our love for God to our love for others?

Think

Interpretation Questions

- Why do you think John talks about love and obedience so much?

- Is love an emotion, an action, or some combination of the two? What is the most common understanding today?

- What do you think it means to "live as Jesus did"? (verse 6)

- Why is it important to live out our faith by loving people? Why do our relationships reflect our relationship with God?

Apply

Application Questions

- What are some ways to love one person you really dislike? If you harbor hatred toward someone, what is one step you can take to begin getting rid of that today?

- John tells us that love is true when it is faithful, when we do what we say we will do. Think about the relationships that are most important to you. How do lies or broken promises affect those relationships in negative ways?

- What are three practical ways you can begin to "live as Jesus did" today?

Do

Optional Activity

Have everyone in your group bring in as many magazines as possible and look at the number of instances where the articles mention love. Then have a discussion on love and what it's really about, and then talk about God's love and how it's different from human love.

QUIET TIME REFLECTIONS

Day 1: 1 John 2:1-2

- What word or phrase jumps out to you? Why?

- Why does John speak of Jesus as the "atoning sacrifice for our sins"? What does "atoning" mean? Is it possible to be sinless for a day?

- Think about some ways Christ has forgiven you for your sins.

Day 2: 1 John 2:3-4

- How does this passage speak to you?

- What commandments do we need to keep in order to know God?

- Think about what it means to really know and follow Jesus.

Day 3: 1 John 2:5-6

- What insight do you gain from this text?

- What does it mean to live like Jesus did?

- Think about some radical ways to live out your faith like Jesus did.

Day 4: 1 John 2:7-8

- What's one question you have about the passage?

- What does this phrase mean: "The darkness is passing and the true light is already shining"?

- Think about what it means to walk in the light and that darkness needs to be acknowledged and called out.

Day 5: 1 John 2:9-10

- What can you learn from this text?

- What relationships do you struggle with that could be bordering on "hate"? Will you consider reconciling with the person and asking God for forgiveness?

- Think about the people you need to talk to because of some hurt or resentment you're holding against them.

Day 6: 1 John 2:11

- What is God saying to you from this verse?

- What are some ways we walk in darkness?

- Think about some practical steps you can take to live in the light.

Day 7: 1 John 2:1-11

Read through the entire passage. Write down the **one verse** that spoke to you the most this week. Commit the verse to memory for an extra challenge!

23. LOVING THE WORLD?
1 John 2:12-29

LEADER'S INSIGHT

From childhood to adulthood, we are all in the process of growing up.

John begins his letter by addressing children in the faith who are trying to understand the basic beliefs of Christianity and want to know how their sins can be forgiven. Then John reminds fathers of their long life of faith. Note the interplay with the phrases that John uses, starting with children in 1 John 2:12, then discussing fathers in verse 13a, and then young men in verse 13b. He continues this same progression in verses 13c-14.

John is making a case that the Word of God has power to help us, however old we are, to overcome the onslaughts of the evil one. Our power and strength to fight temptation and evil does not come from us but through our relationship with Christ and the full reliance upon his Word. At the end of verse 14 John makes this clear: "I write to you young men, because you are strong, and the Word of God lives in you and you have overcome the evil one."

Loving the world or the things of the world is like rooting for the rival of your favorite sports team. John reminds us that the things of the world will pass away (which is probably why, as the old saying goes, you never see U-Haul trucks traveling behind hearses). Encourage students to look at their lives and ask themselves: *What media am I consuming, what brands am I buying, where am I investing my time, passion, and energy?* John's word to us is clear, "Do not love the world or anything in the world. If anyone loves the world, love for the Father is not in them. For everything in the world—the lust of the flesh, the lust of the eyes, and the pride of life—comes not from the Father but from the world. The world and its desires pass away, but whoever does the will of God lives forever." (1 John 2:15-17)

Ultimately, God desires followers who love him and reject the allure of the world. Following Jesus doesn't only mean believing certain things; it involves loving obedience that requires us to reject things that don't honor God. Are we willing to be fully committed followers, or are we just seeking to be part-time Christians who demand a full-time God?

Share

Warm-Up Questions

- What is your favorite sports team? What is that team's rival? Would you ever cheer for the rival team? Why/why not?

- If someone looked at your life, what would he or she say is your first priority?

Observe

Observation Questions

- Read verse 12. Why does John say he's writing to the little children?

- Read verses 15-17. What does John say is "in the world"?

- Read verses 18-25. What is a sign of the last hour?

- Read verse 28. What should the believer continue to do?

Think

Interpretation Questions

- Read verses 12-14. What do you think is the significance of each of the groups included in this section—children, fathers, and young men?

- Read verses 15-17. Why is it better to pursue God more than the world?

- Read verse 28. How does someone abide in Christ? Why is John telling us to do this?

- What is righteousness and what does it mean to practice it, based on verse 29?

Apply

Application Questions

- Why is Scripture so important to our lives, and what disciplines can help insure you continue to grow in reading it?

- In this section, John ties what we believe about Jesus (verses 20-22) with remaining in relationship with Christ and avoiding deception. How can you take steps to grow in your understanding of the beliefs and doctrines of Christianity?

- If "abiding" in Christ involves knowing the truth about God, what are one or two practical things you can do to grow in your knowledge of God?

Do

Optional Activity

Chart an average week. Think in terms of three categories:

- Free time

- Relationships

- Spiritual disciplines (e.g., Bible reading, prayer, serving, giving)

How much time do you spend doing each activity in your week? Does the time you spend reflect more of the world or more of God? What are some things you can do to live a life that reflects more of God?

QUIET TIME REFLECTIONS

Day 1: 1 John 2:12-14

- What word or phrase jumps out to you? Why?

- Why do you think John is addressing children, fathers, and young men?

- What makes us strong? How have you been able to overcome temptation? How important was God's Word in helping you accomplish this?

Day 2: 1 John 2:15-17

- How does this passage speak to you?

- How do you know if you have the love of the Father (God)?

- What will eventually happen to the world and its desires? How does your life reflect the love of God? How are you reflecting the love of worldliness?

Day 3: 1 John 2:18-20

- What insight do you gain from this text?

- According to John, what is a sign we are nearing the last hour? Where do the antichrists come from?

- What knowledge do believers have?

Day 4: 1 John 2:21-25

- What's one question you have about this passage?

- What is the truth that's discussed in verse 21?

- According to John, who is an antichrist?

Day 5: 1 John 2:26-27

- What can you learn from this text?

- Who is John speaking of in verse 26?

- What is the anointing that John talks about?

Day 6: 1 John 2:28-29

- What is God saying to you through these verses?
- What is one way to be confident in Christ?
- What does practicing righteousness look like in your own life? What does it mean to "abide in Christ"? What is one way to abide?

Day 7: 1 John 2:12-29

Read through the entire passage. Write down **one verse** that spoke to you the most this week. Commit the verse to memory for an extra challenge!

24. LOVE OF THE FATHER
1 John 3:1-10

LEADER'S INSIGHT

Think of a time when someone showed love to you.

Perhaps you can think of a parent, a sibling, or a close friend. When someone goes out of his or her way to show love to you, how do you respond? Isn't it natural to want to say thank you, to return the favor in some way?

John is thinking about a similar situation in 1 John 3:1-10 as he turns his attention to the immeasurable love of God for us. Some people wrongly think of God as a wrathful, power-wielding divine being who isn't very warm and friendly. But when John thinks about God, before anything else he wants to talk about God's love for us. (3:1)

John links the love God has for us, as our Father, to our new identities as his adopted children. This is a pretty amazing truth when you think about it. We were completely estranged from God due to our sin, even called enemies of God (Romans 5:10), and yet when we believe in Jesus Christ we are completely forgiven. Now not only are we God's friends, but also we are adopted into his family as his sons and daughters.

So how do we respond to this love? That's what John answers for us in this section. We respond with obedience and love. John gets a bit repetitious here, telling us in verses 4, 5, 6, 7, 8, 9, and 10 that *habitual* sinning is of the devil, but a life of consistent righteousness and love is of Christ. But John isn't trying to give us a checklist of "dos" and "don'ts"; he's saying it's all been "done" for you, what you could never do for yourself. That's love.

Our record of obedience before God is Christ (verse 4), what he has accomplished by his perfect life on our behalf. We are not trying to earn God's love; we can't! Instead, we need to see ourselves as new people, as sons and daughters of God. This new identity changes the way we act and how we treat others. A true son or daughter of God is so thankful that they've been rescued and fully welcomed into God's family that they delight to honor and please God through obedience and love. That's what session 24 is all about: adopted in love by the Father.

Share

Warm-Up Questions

- Do you have any family traditions? Which ones do you like? Which ones don't you like?

- What makes a family? Who is allowed to be a family "member"? Do you have any pets that are considered "family"?

- What are some ways you feel your family's love for you? How do you return love?

Observe

Observation Questions

- Read 3:1. How do we see the love of God for us? Why doesn't the world understand us, according to verse 1?

- Read 3:2-3. Who is the "he" in these verses? How does John say that we purify ourselves, according to verse 3?

- Read 3:4-9. What does John say is the behavior for those who know Jesus versus those who don't know Jesus? What should people be practicing as children of God?

- Read verse 10. According to this verse, how is it evident who are the children of God and who are not?

Think

- Read 3:1-3. What do you think it means to be a child of God? What do you think John means in his phrase "we will be like him" in verse 2?

- Read 3:4-6. What do you think John means when he says, "Makes a practice of sinning"?' Is this different from other types of sinning? According to verse 6, can a life of sin and a life in Jesus exist together? Why not?

- Read 3:7-8. According to John those who practice sin are of whom? And those who practice righteousness are of whom? Why do you think John is using such extreme examples here?

- Read 3:9-10. What does it mean to be born of God? Does John speak of this in any of his other writings? (Hint: John 3.) How is our being children of God evident according to John?

Apply

Application Questions

- Do you need to confess that you have not recognized God's love for you? Have you taken for granted his love for you?

- Is it obvious to others that you are a child of God? Do you fit in with the "world" or do you stand apart?

- Do you make a practice of sinning in any areas in your life? Are you comfortable with something that God says is wrong? Do you dismiss the "little" sins? What do you need to change in your life practices?

- Who do you need to start loving? Is there someone in your life you have wronged and need to apologize to? Is there someone you don't like and you've made that feeling obvious to that person? What "neighbor" do you need to be more loving to?

Do

One of the main questions in this passage is, "Are we practicing righteousness or sinfulness?" This will be a hard exercise even for the brave, but have your students truly evaluate a week in their lives. Ask them to log what they do throughout the week in terms of sinful and righteous activity, and then at the end of the week determine which one they devoted more time to. This is perhaps not a survey they need to share with each other (unless the group trust is built up enough to have proper confession); it's simply meant to be eye-opening for each individual. This also isn't meant as a guilt trip or to make one question equivalent to their salvation as children of God. This is simply an exercise to reveal how they may need to be more intentional about godly practices and disciplines and more on guard against devilish practices. Hopefully this will lead to some genuine repentance.

QUIET TIME REFLECTIONS

Day 1: 1 John 3:1

- What word or phrase jumps out at you? Why?

- How do we know that God loves us? Do you presently feel the love of God for you?

- Have you experienced tension and conflict with others in your life because of your faith in Jesus? According to verse 1 John says that the world didn't know God and therefore won't truly understand us, either. Is that comforting at all to you?

Day 2: 1 John 3:2-3

- How does this passage speak to you?

- When John writes, "what we will be has not yet appeared," he is referring to the fact that one day we will receive new bodies in heaven. What do you think that will be like?

- John says one day Christ will return, and we will see him. What do you think that moment will be like for you?

Day 3: 1 John 3:4-5

- What insight do you gain from this text?

- In your life would you say that you make a practice of sinning? What is the sin you have the hardest time with?

- Do you truly believe that Christ came to take away sins? This not only means that he took away the power of sin over you, but that he offers you forgiveness for your sins. Does that give you hope in overcoming sins in your life?

Day 4: 1 John 3:6

- What's one question you have about this passage?

- What does it mean to abide in Jesus? Look at John 15 for further understanding.

- Why do you think John keeps talking about a child of God not living a life of sin? Does his repetition help you see how serious this is and how opposed to each other these lifestyles are?

Day 5: 1 John 3:7-8

- What can you learn from this text?

- This may be the most serious statement John makes about sinning: "whoever makes a practice of sinning is of the devil." Do you believe that? Do you take sin that seriously in your life?

- What exactly is sin? Why do you think John is spending a lot of time showing not only that righteousness and sin are opposed to each other, but also that they are at war? Are you at war against the sin in your life?

Day 6: 1 John 3:9-10

- What is God saying to you through these verses?

- God's seed in verse 9 can be understood as the Spirit of God, but also the Word of God. Is God's Word in you? Do you need to spend more time reading the Bible? Why is that even important as a child of God?

- Loving other people is part of being a child of God. Do you truly love others in the ways that God loves you? If not, why not?

Day 7: 1 John 3:1-10

Read through the entire passage. Write down **one verse** that spoke to you the most this week. Commit the verse to memory for an extra challenge!

25. LOVE AND HATRED
1 John 3:11-24

LEADER'S INSIGHT

Love one another.

That's the theme for this session: "We should love one another." (verses 11 and 23)

This type of love is not a selfish, self-serving, or easy love, such as when we say, "I love pizza. I love sleeping in. I love my iPhone." John talks about a Christlike love that the world does not understand. We are even warned, "Do not be surprised...if the world hates you." (verse 13)

God sent his only son Jesus Christ to die on the cross for our sins to demonstrate what love looks like. But how should we, as God's children, love others? Verse 18 explains that we should "not love with words or speech but with actions and in truth." This doesn't mean that words don't matter, but that words without actions are meaningless. (For more about faith and deeds read James 2:14-26.)

Although we use words every day, our actions show what we really believe. If we say we care about the poor but never contribute money, food, and supplies or take time to serve the poor, then we are speaking empty words. If we evaluate our words by looking at how we spend our *time and resources,* we will see what we truly value.

The rest of this chapter goes on to explain how we can know if we are Christians. We are told to believe in God's Son, Jesus Christ, and keep his commands—which include loving like Jesus and not hating each other.

In this session students will learn what loving one another looks like by studying the One who shows us how to love.

Share
Warm-Up Questions

- Name three things you love and three things you hate.

- How would you define the word *love*?

- How do you show love for your family and friends?

Observe
Observation Questions

- Read chapter 3, verse 16. How does God show us that he loves us?

- What do verses 17-18 say about how we can show love to others?

- Look at verse 22. What does God ask of us?

- What does verse 24 say about how we can know that God lives in us?

Think
Interpretation Questions

- In verse 13 we are told we should not be surprised that the world hates us. Why would the world hate Christians?

- Read verse 15. Why do you think John says, "Anyone who hates a brother or sister is a murderer" and that "no murderer has eternal life"?

- Look at verses 16-18. What does it mean to "lay down our lives for our brothers and sisters"? Who are our brothers and sisters?

- Read verses 21-22. Do you believe it's possible to "receive from him anything we ask"? Why or why not? What do you think John means here?

Apply

Application Questions

- What does it look like to truly "love one another" and "love with actions and in truth"?

- What should be your response to those who hate or dislike you?

- How have you shown any hatred to others? Is there anyone you have shown hatred toward to whom you need to apologize?

- "Jesus Christ laid down his life for us." Give some practical examples of how you can lay down your life for others.

Do

Optional Activity

Have your group (or each individual) pick one of following activities that would show love to others:

- Sponsor a child from Compassion International or World Vision.

- Organize a food drive for a local food pantry.

- Collect school supplies for needy children.

- Serve meals at a homeless shelter.

- Do chores for elderly people in your community.

- Ask the students for ideas: _____

QUIET TIME REFLECTIONS

Day 1: 1 John 3:11-12

- What word or phrase jumps out to you? Why?

- What led Cain to murder his brother Abel?

- Think about why God has to continually remind us to "love one another." When is it difficult to love others?

Day 2: 1 John 3:13-14

- How does this passage speak to you?

- How do we know "that we have passed from death to life"?

- Think about how you can show love to someone who hates you.

Day 3: 1 John 3:15-16

- What insight do you gain from this text?

- What does it mean if we hate a brother or sister?

- Think about how Jesus shows his love for you. Take time to thank Jesus for all he's done for you and share his love with others.

Day 4: 1 John 3:17-18

- What's one question you have about this passage?

- What does our response to those in need say about our relationship with God?

- Think how you can love "with actions."

Day 5: 1 John 3:19-20

- What can you learn from this text?

- What do you think it means to "belong to the truth"? How do you know if *you* belong to the truth?

- Think about what it means to "rest in his presence." What does this look like in your life?

Day 6: 1 John 3:21-24

- What is God saying to you through these verses?

- What does God command us to do? How well have you been keeping these commands? What changes do you need to make in your life?

- Think about your reasons for pleasing God. Do you ever try to please God to get into heaven or to get him to love you?

Day 7: 1 John 3:11-24

Read through the entire passage. Write down the **one verse** that spoke to you the most this week. Commit the verse to memory for an extra challenge!

26. TEST THE SPIRITS
1 John 4:1-21

LEADER'S INSIGHT

John is writing about the reality of false teachings in his day.

Unfortunately this isn't a problem that has gone away. Today we still need to pay close attention to what's being taught as spiritual truth, to discern truth from error. It doesn't matter if you are in middle school or an older adult: Discernment is vitally important to your spiritual life.

In Deuteronomy chapter 13, God warns his people to be aware of false teachings. That's why it's important for us to know what Christians have believed—the teachings and traditions that have been universally accepted by the church for almost 2,000 years. We call these *doctrines*.

John begins chapter 4 by warning us that we test what is said and taught to see if it truly comes from God (verse 1 NLT). In other words, John is saying, "Don't be gullible. Don't believe everything you hear, and please don't trust every word that comes out of people's mouths." Teens are especially vulnerable to being deceived by bad theology, so as youth workers we need to help them discern between truth and falsehood.

One of the first signs of truth is: *Does the teacher, preacher, or youth worker profess that Jesus is God in the flesh?* John 1:14 says that God took on humanity and was 100 percent man and 100 percent God. If someone teaches that Jesus was only a man or a good moral figure or a great teacher or prophet, John says they are not teaching from God's Spirit. In fact, to deny the deity of Christ is to have the spirit of Antichrist. (verse 3)

The second marker of walking in the truth is living a lifestyle of love. John discusses thoroughly in verses 7-21 that the nature and character of God is love. To live in the Spirit is to love like God. Love is the proof that the Spirit dwells in a believer. Hating others is not a sign of truth, but of falsehood.

The third indicator of knowing the truth is that *Jesus is the Savior of the world.* (verse 14) There have been many great religious leaders over the centuries, but only Jesus Christ is the savior of the world. All things are summed up in Jesus.

Share

Warm-Up Questions

- Of all the school exams and tests you have taken, what was the most difficult?

- Have you ever seen a counterfeit object? How did you know it wasn't real?

- Can you think of any tests you might do to differentiate something that's true from something that's false? Something real from something counterfeit?

Observe

Observation Questions

- Based on verses 1-4, what does the writer say about testing the spirits?

- Read verses 5-10. What message is John sending about God's love?

- In verses 11-15, what do you not understand about the love of Jesus?

- What do we learn about love and fear in verses 16-21?

Think

Interpretation Questions

- Why does John talk about the importance of testing the spirits and false prophets? How might this apply to us today?

- What do you think John means when he says that the one who is in you is greater than the one who is in the world? How is this encouraging?

- What reason does John give for why we love? Why is this order important? What is the difference between loving others *because* God loves us and loving others to *earn* God's love?

Apply

Application Questions

- How do you tell what's real from what's counterfeit? How do you discern truth from error? Can you recognize what is false if you don't know what is true?

- John tells us that fear has to do with punishment. Why do Christians no longer need to fear God's punishment?

- John also tells us that our knowledge of God's love will lead us to live like Jesus, to live a life of love for others. How does loving others remind us that we are loved by God?

Do

Optional Activity

Bring in some articles that describe beliefs of various religious groups (e.g., Jehovah's Witnesses, Mormons, Muslims, Hindus, etc.) Have a conversation about what each group believes and contrast this with biblical Christianity. Remind them what John teaches in this passage—that the best way to recognize what is false is by better knowing what is true. If students have questions, encourage them to further explore the Christian faith, possibly with additional resources.

QUIET TIME REFLECTIONS

Day 1: 1 John 4:1-4

- What word or phrase jumps out to you? Why?

- Why does John warn us not to believe "every spirit but test the spirits"? (verse 1)

- Think about the various false teachings you've heard in the last year. Can you name some?

Day 2: 1 John 4:5-7

- How does this passage speak to you?

- What different viewpoints can you see between worldly teaching and godly teaching?

- Think about how easy it is to be deceived even when reading the Bible.

Day 3: 1 John 4:8-12

- What insight do you gain from this text?

- Why do some non-Christians seem more loving compared to some outspoken Jesus followers?

- Think about people who say they love God but seem indifferent and even hateful toward people.

Day 4: 1 John 4:13-16

- What's one question you have about this passage?

- What does it mean to be "given us of his spirit"? (verse 13)

- Think about the meaning of Jesus as "Savior." What happens to people who don't believe that?

Day 5: 1 John 4:17-19

- What can you learn from this text?
- What fears do you face?
- Think about how love can cast out your fears.

Day 6: 1 John 4:20-21

- What is God saying to you from these verses?
- Why is it easy as a Christian to dislike some people?
- Think about some practical steps to live in love.

Day 7: 1 John 4:1-21

Read through the entire passage. Write down **one verse** that spoke to you the most this week. Commit the verse to memory for an extra challenge!

27. WHAT IS FAITH?
1 John 5:1-12

LEADER'S INSIGHTS

It's good to ask questions.

John in his first epistle is asking the question, "How do we know that we have eternal life?" It's a question we have to ask ourselves, as well as others. Many people, including youth, struggle with the realization of their salvation. "Am I really saved? How do I know?" some might ask.

In chapter 5:1-3, there are a couple of examples John gives that can serve as answers to John's main question above: If we love God and obey his commandments, we have been born of him. While the first seems obvious, obeying his commandments may come as a surprise to some. But it's necessary to realize that from our salvation should spring new life, including obeying God's commandments.

A Christian's faith can be questioned when he or she repeatedly sins and has no change of lifestyle. Inward repentance should be reflected in external actions. Teaching this truth to youth is extremely important. Many of them believe they have made a decision for Christ simply by praying "Jesus come into my heart" when they were little kids. That's the start of the journey, but John is encouraging his readers to grow their faith toward being fully devoted and obedient disciples.

In verses 4-5, the evidence of our faith comes into play, and John writes: "Everyone who has been born of God overcomes the world. And this is the victory that has overcome the world—our faith." What is our faith? The belief that Jesus is the Christ—the Son of God who saved the world from sin and death.

Verses 6-12 describe the testimony of Jesus Christ as the Son of God who saved the world from sin and death. His testimony is that of the divine God; he came not only by water (his baptism) but also by blood (his death on the cross). Not only does Christ's testimony bear witness, but so does the Spirit. (verse 6)

The Father sends the Son to save the world and then sends the Spirit to build up believers. The Spirit bears witness to Christ's work in us. (verse 10) If we reject this witness, we basically are calling God a liar. (verse 11) God's testimony is the life found in his Son. God's formula is pretty simple; those who have the Son are promised life, but those who don't have the Son are left in their own self-righteousness. (verse 12)

Share

Warm-Up Questions

- Share an experience about when you really sensed God's presence.

- Who was the first person to ever tell you about Jesus? What impact did it have on you?

- Have you ever heard a faith story that was really moving? Why was it so impactful?

Observe

Observation Questions

- Read verses 1-3. What does John say about loving God and keeping his commandments? Why are those important?

- Read verses 4-5. What does the writer say about overcoming the world?

- Look at verses 6-8. What does John say about water, blood, and the Holy Spirit?

- Read verses 9-12. What does John say about the importance of a testimony?

Think

- Based on verses 1-3, why do we have to love God *and* obey him? Is our salvation based on works or not? What does Scripture say?

- Read verses 4-5. What does it mean to overcome the world? How does our faith overcome it?

- In verses 6-8 why do you think it's important to have evidence and witnesses?

- Read verses 9-12. What does it mean to make God a liar?

Apply

Application Questions

- How can we practically love God more? How do we get closer to him? How do we learn to obey him? How does his grace play into this?

- After examining the witness of Christ, how does one respond? How should we approach unbelievers who don't "have life"?

- What should we do with the people who say they know God but aren't "living the life"?

Do

Optional Activity

Have the group write out or type their testimonies (i.e., faith stories). Share them with the group and have members discuss and ask questions about each testimony. Encourage students to go home and share the testimonies with their families or parents. Come back next week and ask how their sharing time went.

QUIET TIME REFLECTIONS

Day 1: 1 John 5:1-2

- What word or phrase jumps out to you? Why?
- What does it mean to be "born of God"?
- List some ways that you have been disobedient to God. Seek repentance and ask God how you can improve in these areas.

Day 2: 1 John 5:3-4

- How does this passage speak to you?
- Why do we feel as though God's commands are burdensome? How can we change our thinking?
- How did salvation happen for you? How has change happened for you in your Christian life? Slow? Fast?

Day 3: 1 John 5:5-6

- What insight do you gain from this text?
- What does it mean to believe that Jesus is the Son of God? How do we believe?
- What does John mean when he says, "he came by water and blood"? How does this testify to Christ's greatness?

Day 4: 1 John 5:7-8

- What's one question you have about this passage?
- Why is having the testimony of the three such a big deal?
- How have you seen the evidence of Christ and the Spirit in your life?

Day 5: 1 John 5:9-10

- What can you learn from this text?

- What does John mean when he says, "whoever does not believe God has made him a liar"?

- Why does John say "the testimony of God is greater"? What does this mean?

Day 6: 1 John 5:11-12

- What is God saying to you through these verses?

- Think about your testimony. Are you experiencing the life that God offers? Why or why not?

- Think about the fact that some people have life and some don't. Has God placed on your heart any of your friends who don't know Jesus? How can you share the testimony of Christ with them?

Day 7: 1 John 5:1-12

Read through the entire passage. Write down the **one verse** that spoke to you the most this week. Commit the verse to memory for an extra challenge!

28. ETERNAL LIFE
1 John 5:13-21

LEADER'S INSIGHT

Can anyone really *know* if they are going to heaven?

The book of 1 John highlights several differences between those who are children of God and those who are children of the world. John reminds us there is a difference between those who walk in light and those who walk in darkness. (1 John 1:5-10) Those he addresses in his letter have seen people leave their fellowships—people they thought were real followers of Christ. (1 John 2:19) John affirms that those who remain belong to Christ and urges them to continue loving one another.

John gives us a wonderful affirmation of why he has written his letter in John 5:13: "I write these things to you who believe in the name of the Son of God so that you may *know* that you have eternal life." Did you catch that emphasis? John believes that we can actually KNOW if we are going to heaven! The logical question is "How?" This is where the context of verse 13 is helpful. If we back up one sentence to verse 12, we read, "He who has the Son has life; he who does not have the Son of God does not have life." We can know we have eternal life by whether or not we have Jesus Christ, whether or not we have put our hope and trust in him. 1 John 5:1 tells us, "Everyone who believes that Jesus is the Christ is born of God." If we believe that Jesus is our Savior and we love him, then he is our life. We know that we have eternal life because we belong to him.

Then John moves from confidence in our salvation to confidence in answered prayer. 1 John 5:14-15 (which are great memory verses) tell us that we can have confidence that *any prayer* offered in accordance with God's will is granted! That's the kind of truth that makes you want to stop reading and start praying.

Finally, we are encouraged to pray for those who struggle with sin, which includes just about everyone! John indicates that there are two kinds of people who struggle with sin. There are legitimate Christians who make sinful choices (5:16-18). While these sins will not ultimately lead to death (i.e., hell), these choices are not pleasing to God and can negatively affect their relationship with God and others. There are also those who do not know Christ who sin in a way that leads to death. Some may claim to know Christ, but the only way to really discern who is a real Christian from who is not is to see the fruit of their choices over a lifetime of faithfully following Jesus. Anyone can claim to be a Christian, but true believers will consistently grow in love, joy, and other fruits of the Spirit. As John reminds us, "anyone born of God does not continue to sin." (verse 18)

Share
Warm-Up Questions

- Would you describe yourself as a spiritual person? Why or why not?

- What is one question you'd like to ask God?

- What is something you see in the world that really frustrates you?

Observe
Observation Questions

- Read verse 13. What does John tell us we can "know"? According to this verse, does eternal life begin now, or do we have to wait until after we die?

- Look at verses 14-15. What confidence can we have?

- Verses 16-18 describe sin that does not lead to death (committed by Christians). What are we instructed to do if we see Christians sinning?

- In verses 19-21, what "understanding" has Jesus given to his followers?

Think

Interpretation Questions

- Look at verse 13. Why should this verse be a huge encouragement to Christians?

- Read verses 14-15. Why do some of our prayers go unanswered?

- Look at verses 16-18. Why should we pray for Christians who are sinning?

- In verses 19-21, why do you think John keeps using the word *know*?

Apply

Application Questions

- Would you say you "know" you're going to heaven? Why or why not?

- How can we make sure our prayers line up with God's will? How should we respond when we feel like we're praying God's will but nothing seems to happen?

- What can a person do who's struggling with an area of sin in his or her life to fight against that sin? What is a practical step to take to begin resisting the sin?

- What is an idol? How do we keep ourselves from idols?

Do

Optional Activity

Have each person in the group come up with one particular area (person, issue, or country) where God's will needs to be done. Talk about what you think God's will might look like if he answered that prayer immediately. Have one person in the group read aloud 1 John 5:14-15. Now have the group take the area they mentioned and pray briefly for God's will to be done. After you finish praying, have someone read aloud 1 John 5:14-15.

QUIET TIME REFLECTIONS

Day 1: 1 John 5:13

- What word or phrase jumps out to you? Why?

- Were you aware that someone can "know" whether or not they will have eternal life? Do you know that you have eternal life or do you have doubts? Is there someone you need to talk to about this?

- Do you have friends or family members who are wrestling with whether or not they'll go to heaven when they die? Would this verse be an encouragement to them? Is there a way that you can share this verse with them?

Day 2: 1 John 5:14-15

- How does this passage speak to you?

- Do you believe that God answers our prayers? Have you ever prayed what you thought was God's will but nothing seemed to happen? What could be going on in that circumstance?

- How can we know God's will in any particular circumstance? If we can't know God's will specifically, can we know it generally? How should that affect our prayers?

Day 3: 1 John 5:16-17

- What insight do you gain from this text?

- Do you know of anyone who claims to be a Christian but is struggling with sin? Have you been praying for that person? Are you that person? Have you asked people to pray for you?

- We read that "all wrongdoing is sin." Is there any "wrongdoing" in your life that you haven't been taking seriously as sin? If so, what decision do you need to make in that area?

Day 4: 1 John 5:18

- What's one question you have about this passage?

- Think about someone you respect as a Christian. What is it about the way that person lives that you respect? How does that person respond to temptation and sin?

- This verse mentions two people "born of God"—referring to a Christian and Jesus. What do you think it means that Jesus "keeps him safe" and "the evil one cannot harm him"?

Day 5: 1 John 5:19

- What can you learn from this text?

- How can people know they are "children of God"?

- What does "the whole world is under the control of the evil one" mean? What are examples of this truth?

Day 6: 1 John 5:20-21

- What is God saying to you from these verses?

- What do you think John means when he calls Jesus "him who is true"? How is that an encouragement to God's people?

- Why do we need to keep ourselves from "idols"? Are there any idols in your life? If so, have you prayed and asked God to remove them? What needs to be your next step?

Day 7: 1 John 5:13-21

Read through the entire passage. Write down the **one verse** that spoke to you the most this week. Commit the verse to memory for an extra challenge!

29. GRACE, MERCY, AND PEACE
2 John

LEADER'S INSIGHT

The letter of 2 John is brief in length but not in substance.

It has a similar feeling to that of 1 John. Although short in verses (only 12), it's rich in depth. The apostle urges two attributes in us: truth and love. Through all the letters of John, we see many contrasts: Light and darkness, new and old commandments, loving God and loving the world, love and fear, and the Christ and the antichrist.

The contrast of truth and love is one of the main themes of 2 John. Balancing truth and love is not easy. If we focus on the extreme of "truth," we are vulnerable to being judgmental, legalistic, and narrow in our views. If we err on the side of "love" only, then we open ourselves up to the possibility of having no absolutes or objective reality. John wants his readers to *balance* truth and love. Why is John concerned?

False teachers had been around for a long time, and John addresses this issue. The apostle Paul also wrote of this danger in Titus 1:10-11: "For there are many rebellious people, mere talkers and deceivers, especially those of the circumcision group. They must be silenced, because they are ruining whole households by teaching things they ought not teach—and that for the sake of dishonest gain."

2 John opens from "The Elder" which most likely is "code" language associated with the author, John the apostle. He is writing to the "chosen lady and her children" which may be a message to the local gathering of believers who were allowing and following false teachings—or possibly to a specific person, a literal woman.

John begins by fighting for the truth of God and adds the popular greeting or benediction: Grace, mercy and peace from God the Father and from Jesus Christ. (verse 3) John is thrilled to discover that the people he has invested in are still "walking in the truth." (verse 4) One of the great joys in youth ministry is seeing students "walk the walk" in high school, college, and adulthood. It's also sad to see the ones who do not run the race for the long haul.

Teens need to know that loving God is more than emotion, a spiritual high at a retreat or summer beach camp. Loving God is "walking in obedience to his commandments. As you have heard from the beginning, his command is that you walk in love." (verse 6)

Truth and love go together, but we must warn students and families that "Many deceivers, who do not acknowledge Jesus Christ as coming in the flesh, have gone out into the world. Any such person is the deceiver and the antichrist." (verse 7)

In this session we learn three insights: We stand strong by God's grace. We live under Christ's mercy. We walk in the peace of God.

Share
Warm-Up Questions

- Where do people look for truth in today's world?

- How do you know if you really love someone?

- What is it like to both love and obey someone?

Observe
Observation Questions

- Based on verses 1-4, what do you think the author means by "truth" and "the truth"?

- Read verses 5-7. What is taught about truth and love?

- In verse 8, what is the writer saying in regard to not following the teachings of Christ?

- What do we learn from verses 9-12? Does this seem a little harsh?

Think

Interpretation Questions

- Why does John focus so much on truth and deception? What does that mean for today's world?

- What do you think John means in verse 11:"Anyone who welcomes him shares in his wicked work"? (See verse 10 for understanding the context.)

- Why is it important to walk in the truth you have? How does it impact others when we don't live out our faith? Would your friends and family say you are walking in the faith?

Apply

Application Questions

- How are you doing on a scale of 1 (poor) to excellent (10) with this statement? "I am consistent on living out my faith in front of others."

- What are some practical ways to demonstrate love to people who are not walking in the truth?

- What are some false teachings you have heard that conflict with the Christian lifestyle?

- How can you protect yourself from falling prey to false teachings?

Do

Optional Activity

Have your group study some religions that may be different from Christianity. Ask each group member to choose a particular religion and give the group a chance to come back with the answers to three questions:

- What does this religion believe regarding who Jesus is?

- What is their view of salvation (how does one become right with God)?

- **What is their standard of truth (some book, the Bible, others)?** Possible faiths to examine: Judaism, Hinduism, Mormonism, Jehovah's Witness, Islam, Buddhism, etc.

QUIET TIME REFLECTIONS

Day 1: 2 John 1-2

- What word or phrase jumps out to you? Why?

- Why does the writer spend so much time on "truth"? Why is "truth" important?

- Think about some ways you practice and don't practice living in the truth.

Day 2: 2 John 3-4

- How does this passage speak to you?

- Why do you think the writer starts with "grace, mercy, and peace?" What do these terms mean?

- Think about what sort of joy you experience when you see a friend come to faith in Jesus.

Day 3: 2 John 5-6

- What insight do you gain from this text?

- What does it mean to walk in obedience?

- Think about some of the ways we turn people off from following Christ when we don't live in the truth.

Day 4: 2 John 7-8

- What's one question you have about this passage?

- What does it mean to be deceived?

- Think about what this verse means when you "lose what you have worked for?" Is the author saying we can lose our salvation in Christ?

Day 5: 2 John 9

- What can you learn from this text?

- What is the meaning of "whoever continues in the teaching has both the Father and the Son" and how does it work?

- Think about some people you know who perhaps have walked away from the faith. Pray for them that the Father might bring them back to himself.

Day 6: 2 John 10-12

- What is God saying to you from these verses?

- What are we asked to do when someone rejects the teaching of Christ?

- Think about some of the times you've sent someone a note (email or text) and it may have been better to have spent time with them instead.

Day 7: 2 John 1-12

Read through the entire passage. Write down the **one verse** that spoke to you the most this week. Commit the verse to memory for an extra challenge!

30. CLOSING THOUGHTS
3 John

LEADER'S INSIGHT

Great authors know how to drive home their points.

John is such a writer. In this third letter, he refers to himself as "The Pastor." (MSG) 2 John was written to a "lady," and 3 John is directed to a man. John writes his good friend Gaius, a familiar name in the Roman Empire, wishing him the best of health and "good fortune" and to prosper in "everyday affairs." (MSG)

Ever had a good friend who poured his or her life into yours? Or perhaps you have been that friend to someone else—giving yourself to someone you deeply care about. That's what is going on here between John and Gaius, and it's an example of true godly Christian friendship.

John begins by exhorting Gaius that true friendship and hospitality is actually a "visible" demonstration of the faith. How we treat people matters, and non-Christians looking for truth should not need to look farther than Christ-followers who manifest love.

Jesus told his followers to love one another, and that love is *the* sign of knowing if we are Christians or not. In John's third letter, he encourages Gaius to not be quick to judge, rather to be hospitable. In John's day, there were many itinerant speakers (apostles, prophets, teachers, and evangelists) who were on the move to share Jesus and establish new church plants. In their day, as in our day, occasionally there would be some fabulous communicator who would come to town with some weird theology. John warns to test the spirits and the content of their messages. He also encourages Gaius to love those who bring the message of the gospel in a manner worthy of the kingdom.

There is a second person mentioned in this short letter named Diotrephes. (verses 9-11) This man was selfish, apparently accusing John with "wicked words" and excommunicating people from the church. John rebukes Diotrephes, but a man by the name of Demetrius is affirmed (verse 12) as having a good reputation with everyone. Usually when there was conflict in the early church, someone of integrity was sent to "clear the air" and make things right. In this scenario, it was Demetrius. What kind of character and integrity do you have? Are you a Diotrephes or a Demetrius in the way you deal with people?

Share
Warm-Up Questions
- How would you define integrity?
- Whom do you look up to who has great character and integrity?
- What does it take to become a person of great integrity?

Observe
Observation Questions
- Based on the first five verses, why is the author concerned about Gaius?
- Read verses 6-8. What do you learn about Gaius?
- In verses 9-11, what is Diotrephes' problem?
- What do we learn from verses 12-13 about Demetrius?

Think
Interpretation Questions
- Why does John focus on affirming Gaius?

- Why are encouragement and affirmation so important to give and receive?

- Why do you think John is upset with Diotrephes?

- What do Proverbs 11:2, 16:5, and 29:1 say about pride and arrogance?

Apply

Application Questions

- How are you doing on a scale of 1 (poor) to excellent (10) with this statement: "I am a person of integrity"?

- What are some practical ways to live out humility?

- What are some steps you can take in order to avoid becoming like Diotrephes?

- How can you protect yourself from being critical and pessimistic?

Do

Optional Activity

Have everyone in your group send an email, text, or "real letter" to two people. First, send a letter of encouragement to a friend, mentor, or someone who has inspired you to live a life of godliness and integrity, and tell this person how he or she has impacted your life.

The second letter is to someone you are concerned about, perhaps who's moved away from the faith or is struggling with resentment, doubt, or hurt. Encourage that person to know that God loves him or her very much and wants him or her to reconnect with Jesus.

QUIET TIME REFLECTIONS

Day 1: 3 John 1-2

- What word or phrase jumps out to you? Why?

- What does John pray for here?

- Think about someone today who needs this exact prayer—and then lift that person up to God.

Day 2: 3 John 3-4

- How does this passage speak to you?

- What is John excited about here in this passage?

- Think about how happy you are when someone you love walks with God. Pray a blessing on that person today.

Day 3: 3 John 5-6

- What insight do you gain from this text?

- Whom do you know who really loves God? How does that person impact you?

- Think about some of your friends who have fallen away from fellowship with other Christians. Take a moment to ask God to bring them back.

Day 4: 3 John 7-8

- What is one question you have about this passage?

- What does it mean to have godly standards?

- Think about your standards in your walk with Jesus. Which of these are negotiable and which are nonnegotiable?

Day 5: 3 John 9-11

- What can you learn from this text?

- What is the meaning of "loving to be first among them"? Have you ever been accused of loving to be first?

- Think about some people who are self-serving and self-absorbed. Pray for them today without condemning them.

Day 6: 3 John 12-14

- What is God saying to you through these verses?

- Why are we told that Demetrius has a good testimony? What does that mean?

- Think about what people think about you. Are you respected? Admired? Viewed as a hypocrite? How do people view you?

Day 7: 3 John 1-14

Read through the entire passage. Write down the **one verse** that spoke to you the most this week. Commit the verse to memory for an extra challenge!

ACKNOWLEDGMENTS

One of the great and special joys I have as a professor of Youth Ministry, Family, and Culture at Columbia International University (C.I.U.) is teaching and mentoring quality students. I get to rub shoulders with some individuals who are exceptionally gifted in working with teens, college students, and families.

This is my third *Studies On the Go* book, part of a series originally developed by Laurie Polich Short. The first two I wrote were *Proverbs* and *Philippians, Colossians, and First and Second Thessalonians*. I encouraged (and sometimes begged) some of my students to write because I believe God can use these resources.

It "takes a village" to write a book, and so a huge thanks goes to my writing and research team. Even though I am the primary writer and editor (the one with his name on the book cover and the chapters not mentioned below), you should know that there were many who contributed in some way to this volume. All of the contributors attended and graduated from Columbia International University, with the exception of my wife Rhonda who serves as a faculty grader. Their voices can be heard and seen in the chapters listed below. Thank you for your insights, observations, and questions on James, 1 and 2 Peter, and 1-3 John. I appreciate your writing contributions. Well done!

- Tyler Byler, Youth Worker: Chapters 4 and 9

- Matt Densky, Director of Student Ministries: Chapters 16 and 24

- Karen Grant, Professor: Chapter 5 and 25

- Howard Ki, Youth Pastor: Chapter 19

- Chris Leiby, Pastor: Chapters 15 and 23

- Dustin McGriff, Student Ministries: Chapter 18

- Trevor Miller, Director of Worship Production and Young Adults: Chapters 3 and 17

- Rachel Olshine, College Counselor: Chapter 6

- Rhonda Olshine, College Educator: Chapter 13
- Jeff Philpott, Lead Pastor: Chapter 8, 14, 28
- Jacob Tedder, Minister of Youth: Chapters 7 and 27